Understanding the silent communication of dogs

Second Edition

By Rosie Lowry
In association with Marilyn Aspinall

Foreword by Sheila Harper

Contents

Foreword

by professional dog trainer, behaviour counsellor and teacher of canine behaviour – Sheila Harper

The age of awareness, true respect and empathy has arrived at last! Rosie clearly understands dogs, their behaviour and interactions and, as a result, knows how to promote the very best for families and professionals, dogs as individuals and also the general public.

Interacting with dogs on a daily basis and working through their issues, along with her own, has given Rosie a sound foundation and an insight into dogs that few are ever privileged to achieve. She has developed a common-sense yet critical approach. She has adopted a fundamental dog and owner – centred stance, evaluating each as an individual, and is unwavering in her effort to help owners meet their dogs' needs. It should become very apparent to every reader that she lives her philosophy!

Rosie guides the reader towards knowledge that will help to unlock the door to better observation and an understanding into the real canine world, rather than the one that tends to come from interpretation as opposed to observation. Helping the reader to develop such a special perception can, for those who are ready, open the way to a whole new world.

One of Rosie's greatest strengths is the fact that she has made and acknowledged her own mistakes, has come to terms with them, learnt from them and then applied this learning to help prevent others from a similar fate. Another strength is that she has the knowledge to draw parallels between species, particularly canine and human. From communication to emotion, stress to life values, she shows the reader how to gain a greater empathy with others.

Few ever consider how to build a relationship. Frequently we read or hear about how to be the dog's leader or how to gain respect (often a euphemism for the words fear or control), but rarely are we given accurate information about how specifically to develop a good relationship with our dogs. Trust and understanding are key, replacing the more common ideas of commands and control. This book shows that finding the right balance and being in a stable, mutually beneficial relationship with the dog promotes appropriate, sensible behaviour. Such behaviour is based on encouraging choice along with allowing the dog space to grow and mature. Surely this is much more preferable than the tendency towards dogs becoming owner-reliant as is the case with a large number of over-trained dogs today?

Why do I feel that this book is so important? At its core it contains valuable information for each one of us, including the dog, and even increases our understanding of other species.

For the individual, family or professional, it provides an opportunity to begin to see the dog as a being in its own right, with emotions and an ability to communicate far beyond the vocalisation that most consider to be their main means of interaction. It shows how problems can be prevented simply by altering the angle from which the dog is viewed and changing approaches. It helps us understand more about why the dog displays certain aspects of behaviour: that they are usually in response to human demands or our own limitations and lack of awareness. This book also encourages us not to look only at the symptoms but to start the journey towards a more holistic approach, where identifying and dealing with the underlying cause will have far reaching implications: improvement and balance for life rather than a quick fix that can result in the dog developing health issues or even more deep-seated behavioural problems.

In addition we need to consider the demands we place upon the dog in daily life; to understand that putting them into situations we haven't yet given them the skills to deal with is likely to lead to misunderstanding and conflict.

This of course, is bound to be of benefit for the dog. Canine instincts may not always be compatible with human ideals. Therefore to be understood, valued as an individual, and acknowledged and accepted for the species it is, complete with those instincts, has to be a big step forward. Such acceptance brings about security and promotes calmness and balance. The boundaries Rosie suggests are not about heavy-handed "leadership", but, if employed correctly, will encourage self-esteem and life-skills, promoting mature, sensible behaviour.

So how does this affect the general public? Where a dog has the skills and ability to recognise his own limits, to exercise self-control and to be able to take himself out of situations he knows are too much for him, ensures that he is less likely to have to respond to conflict or confrontation. The outcome of responsible dog ownership is society's acceptance. In an age where the anti-dog lobby is having an ever-stronger voice, the consequences on the general public arising from applying Rosie's suggestions could lead to important changes in attitude, reflecting greater tolerance and potentially even approval.

Rosie has studied widely, reading literature, attending courses and learning from humans, and more importantly, learning from the animals themselves. By putting theories into practice and testing her beliefs, she has gained a deeper appreciation of which are of value and which can be discarded. Her down-to-earth approach is an asset that she brings to every aspect of her daily life. She gives the reader ideas of how to make changes, how to work and how to help dogs along with reasons behind those suggestions. She provides motivation for us all, encouraging a better understanding rather than a simple recipe. Passionate yet sophisticated, the simplicity of her words belies her understanding. The benefits of this approach are verified by outright success.

Enjoy, learn, and appreciate the universal value of applying this philosophy.

Sheila Harper B. Ed., BA

Sheila is the well known and highly respected principal of the International Programme for Applied Canine Studies. She has lectured in the USA and New Zealand and currently teaches students on a broad range of aspects relating to canine behaviour and communication, throughout Europe, while continuing to work with problematic dogs in rescue kennels and homes.

Introduction

Every scenario, dog and owner is unique. This book has been written to encourage owners and people working with dogs to think about what they are doing and why they are doing it. It was composed for the dog's sake, but also to offer help to the owner who is struggling with their dog's behaviour and health. We very often accept advice concerning our dogs from too many sources and act without taking much else into consideration. I used to be like that until I realised I was creating more problems for my dogs than solving them. Although they weren't happy, like many other dogs, they tolerated it until it became an issue for me. It never occurred to me that there might be a problem for them before I was affected directly but, looking back, I now realise my dogs weren't comfortable with much of what I expected of them. Then I had a Mastiff, and that brought things to my attention in a BIG way. Believe me, you have to do something when you are the carer (because that's what we are for dogs we have living with us) for a Mastiff with a problem!

However, I wonder just how many dogs struggle to get their message across to us, especially the smaller breeds. It is not possible to look at all aspects of behaviour from every angle and suggest training to suit each dog's situation. This is why it is important to take the information in this book and use it as a basis for improving your awareness. For further help, see the contacts at the end of the book.

We are all influenced by what we experience and, to my way of thinking, it would be really helpful for dog owners to have knowledge of this way of 'being' with dogs before deciding what they 'do' with them. I hope the information I am offering will help many dogs be better understood by owners / carers and encourage them to want to find out even more about dogs.

Because this is an holistic approach and considers all elements of the dog's life, not just the visible problems, it is inevitable that there will be some cross-over within the book as many aspects have a knock-on effect and are components to be considered when trying to alter different behaviour issues. Therefore, some information will appear in more than one chapter as it will be relevant to several areas of concern. I think that knowledge of the key elements influencing canine behaviour is highly important and I would like as many people to be aware of and understand them as possible.

I no longer teach my dogs tricks such as sitting, lying down, weaving, walking to heel etc as I feel that is imposing my wants and needs onto the dog.

I try to look at it from the dogs' point of view and consider how they might interpret what I am asking of them and whether it's appropriate for that particular dog. If I believe it is, I then question how can I possibly achieve my aim in a way that the dog is most likely to learn something. I decide on the most plausible approach for the dog, where he can be happy to learn because that offers a higher chance of a positive result for both of us. It can become addictive for us to ask an animal to do something and they obey; their compliance makes us feel good, so we keep on asking: I felt great when telling a dog to sit, down and stay and he did it without hesitation. We are proud of our dogs and having control over them can build our self-esteem. Unfortunately though, it can actually detract from theirs so we need to be aware of what is happening.

Society seems to like to see a dog doing as he is told, even though in many instances control per se may not be needed, but the more control we apply the less equipped the dog is to make choices for himself; thus our self-esteem grows and that of the dogs diminishes and they become ever more reliant on us directing them.

Without awareness of canine communication, how can we know what is going on inside the dog's mind and body? However, we can easily by-pass any concerns on this by getting hooked on having control over our dogs, with the feel-good factor rewarding us every time we demonstrate it.

Sometimes we don't even question what we are doing with dogs, we do it because others are and maybe because we know of no alternative but does the dog appreciate why we want them to sit, down, stay, heel and so forth? Does it make any sense to them?

What are we looking for? It might be harder for people but fairer for the dog to seek out what lies behind the commands and examine the reasons why we want our dog to act in this manner. I am asking you to think it through instead of simply telling a dog what to do.

Repetitive commands requiring these actions to be performed over and over again can take a toll on their body and mind too. How can a dog tell you he is uncomfortable in a certain position or that every time he tries to sit it hurts somewhere, if you don't recognise his language? Kaos, my first mastiff, suddenly rebelled and would not sit. She'd been doing what she was asked every time until one particular day she refused. Later we found her to have cruciate ligament problems in her legs and had probably been very uncomfortable for months in many of the positions I had repeatedly commanded, not to mention negotiating the slippery floor in the training hall every week. I thought she was being stubborn but dogs will have reasons for doing or not doing things and are seldom obstinate just for the sake of it. Perhaps we might learn to listen and adapt to making their life fairer. Like most successful relationships, it's about give and take, as well as understanding. Think about how you relate to your best friends. When you apply the same approach to your dog, you reap the reward intrinsically; gaining satisfaction from working with him, not just imposing your will upon him.

Over time, with repeated application of control and lack of choice, dogs can actually lose the ability to make rational decisions becoming totally reliant on us telling them what to do, when and how.

Giving dogs choices builds their confidence. If we set boundaries for them, with appropriate space and time in which to act, the resultant learning is less superficial as they have been involved in some of the decision making at moments when they are ready to do so. Dogs can learn to problem-solve for themselves.

In my experience most owners think it is important for their dogs to be able to deal with life while retaining their character too. I was considered pretty effective at training my dogs, so helped others to train theirs but when I started to challenge my views on what I was doing and why I wanted my dogs to follow commands, I soon realised there was very little that was actually necessary or useful in real life situations or served a practical purpose. Kaos became fearful of dogs and people (a story for later – socialisation). I taught her to go behind me so I could be a barrier for her when people or dogs were coming toward us while out walking and to 'watch' so keeping her focus on me.

Kaos was great and did what was expected every time except when there was someone heading our way. Of course she couldn't watch me, she had to pay attention to what scared her.

Imagine; could you focus on someone else while something scary was heading towards you? Kaos would just go to pieces and couldn't cope making her appear to be a dangerous dog when, in truth, she was simply scared and dealt with it by lunging and barking at people and dogs invading her personal space. The extent of that space will vary with the individual and may be different from day to day but, due to past experiences, Kaos needed quite a large space most of the time.

When I changed my methods and looked at Kaos' reasons for responding this way and began to gain her trust by not demanding or expecting so much from her, she started to feel safer. It took some time until she had sufficient confidence in me to trust that I had learnt another way of dealing with her environment. We worked together slowly, in a more natural way, initially not getting too close to what spooked her until she was ready to advance. This took some months. When a dog has a problem, the focus we put on it can tend to make matters worse, so, having realised Kaos had an issue, reading her communication helped me to recognise when it was appropriate to teach her and when it was not. We feel differently some days to others, as do animals, and I found that we had greater success in training if Kaos' feelings were taken into account.

Many dogs do what is asked of them, regardless of whether their feelings are considered, but I prefer working in a way that ensures the dog's best interests are met by going at their pace and with empathy for them. Not only that but, from time to time, I consider it important to look again at what I am doing with my dogs and just re-evaluate it.

When we have a dog that performs or readily complies with commands there's a tendency to ask more of him. It is tempting to take him with us to all sorts of places without thinking about the effect it may have. However, internally, stress responses and changes in body chemistry will be taking place as the dog tries to cope with these challenges; not what was intended I'm sure. So again, before teaching a dog to carry out certain behaviours, always question whether it is worth it and why we are doing it; is it for the dog or for us?

Many dogs will work for food; it is the most commonly used motivator. However, because we control their access to this vital resource, they rely on us for their very existence; what a moral responsibility we have! Unwittingly, parents can create food issues for their children; using it to console an upset youngster, to reward desired behaviour, to distract, prevent, or interrupt unwanted behaviour, even as a means of showing affection and, by withholding it, to punish. It is my belief that the way we use food with our dogs may result in problems for some of them too; what is happening in their brains when they are faced with something they truly fear together with a piece of juicy chicken? There is conflict. Do they take the food or not? Sadly many dogs will take the food, especially when hungry or are food obsessed due to past experiences, even though they are being pushed to the limit. In other words, I know that I can coerce dogs to perform to my commands despite their emotional state but I have chosen not to do this any longer.

It was scary for me to change and abandon my props but I haven't looked back since and am confident that my dogs are truly happier. They had seemed so eager to learn, alert and attentive, which I saw as enjoyment of training but I wonder, were they just working out what to do to be fed?

Often we try to command a dog when we are worried about the way he might act or what other people think about us but now my approach is to look at the situation, think why the dog might behave in that way, weigh up the options and make a decision based on my conclusions. The dog may be in a position to begin learning straight away or perhaps other things need putting in place first. What I have learnt is that working in this way has far longer lasting effects, strengthens the relationship between dog and carer and is beneficial to the dog – he learns for himself at his own pace.

Simply managing the symptoms doesn't address the emotions behind the behaviour. Dogs do need to be taught to do things but it's more a matter of how and when, as well as knowing why we do it. What we teach ought to make sense to the dog. Consider this common scenario – at the roadside, owner asks for the dog to sit. This is what I used to do every time we came to a kerb, regardless of the conditions. Do we know how it feels for our dog to sit on a wet pavement? Some breeds would find this so uncomfortable; surely a 'wait' would suffice? Now I make a compromise allowing the dog to choose his position while he waits until it is safe to proceed and all is fine.

Asking a dog to do something and using food, praise or a toy may be a quick way of achieving results but it initiates emotion within the dog. Teaching a dog something while limiting his chances of getting into trouble by applying a boundary (taking into consideration his skill levels and whether what we are teaching is realistic) enables the dog to find his own way of doing what we want and we support him with guidance relating to the communication he shows.

For example; if you ask a dog to 'wait' while a boundary, long line, car door or similar, is in place, over time, he learns what 'wait' means. He doesn't need rewarding for this as 'the penny dropping' provides an intrinsic reward; it is self satisfying. This might sound controversial but the significance to the dog of any reward we offer is something to think about.

I'm sure you have discovered that dogs learn well from watching what is going on and we can give them relevant opportunities to do so. Incidental learning works for them just as it does for us; they can learn things for themselves if given the chance. We can apply some limitations e.g. barriers or other boundaries and within these confines they are free to make choices. That way we find we no longer need to use so many commands. People are intelligent enough to work out how to make it possible for the dog to have appropriate opportunities to learn.

Pogo, a fairly recent addition to our family, is a border collie cross who has had some bad experiences in her life and she occasionally finds it hard to accept Hagrid, my current mastiff. One such time is when we are together in the lounge during the evening. If she is in there first, she lunges and barks, snapping in Hagrid's face as he enters the room. One way I have found to help her feel safer is to put her on a long line which my husband holds as he sits on the settee next to her thus increasing her sense of security. Another option that works is for Hagrid to come into the lounge first. He quickly settles and dozes off, then Pogo comes in and usually, after a short time lies down either on the settee or the floor, just a few feet away from Hagrid, and goes into a deep sleep too.

Sometimes she or Hagrid chooses to settle in the adjoining room which is fine by us. Pogo makes some choices about where she wants to be and it's up to us to help and support her decisions regarding what she has to do to feel safe. In addition, by using barriers, Hagrid has been taught not to invade her space. It works really well and gives Pogo confidence that her needs will be catered for.

Training in this way means working with the dog while adapting to suit the situation and dogs involved. If something doesn't work we find something that does. Both dogs learn from it and so do we. I'm sure that the intrinsic reward I feel from achieving a harmonious result is shared by the dogs too. Using food, praise, or play would only add excitement to what is a delicate situation and could wipe out the progress made. It is lifelong learning that a dog can take into other situations as and when they present themselves, so continuing to build up their confidence.

I firmly believe in teaching dogs social etiquette, an important factor in any society and imperative for their survival in the surroundings they occupy, enabling all to get along in harmony. It is essential for our dogs to learn where the boundaries are, what is and what is not acceptable. I also feel it is important for us to learn dogs' boundaries and respect them equally. In addition, by building up a practical, balanced relationship with your dog, you will construct a basis for training such techniques as recall. Encouraging the dog to want to be with you, rather than demanding that they come, will be much easier. I employ boundaries, but give the dog choices within them, making sure that I do not take a negative line when I am interacting with them. No nagging, bad temper or using aversive methods, which may create insecurity, but just setting things up so that the dog gets it right by himself. I do not punish unwanted behaviour, I simply ignore it while remaining open and available to the dog. If you are consistently positive with your dog, he will learn to trust you.

N.B. In the text, when the gender of a dog is unknown it will be referred to as "he", to keep things simple.

Vocal Communication

Communication is a huge topic and, in this book, I have focussed on the non-vocal side of the subject. Although I have only scratched the surface, hopefully it will get you started on thinking about what your dog is saying.

Vocalisation is a further area to consider (perhaps requiring a book of its own). However any vocal communication your dog offers is significant and, as it contributes to the whole situation, it needs to be taken into account when assessing matters.

Using the information in this book, developing your observational skills and becoming more familiar with dogs will provide a good basis for studying vocal communication too.

When dogs have to resort to vocalising such as whining, howling, yelping, barking, growling or snarling, they are far more likely to get a reaction from people, than if they stay quiet. Making a noise can be very effective, as people generally take notice, but the outcome may work against the dog at times, possibly resulting in their euthanasia if their communication is taken as aggression.

That is why I have prioritised informing people about the non verbal language so that dogs have a chance of being understood without having to make their point too loudly.

The basis of shared relationships

Understanding the dog by putting ourselves into their position is the best thing we can do for them in the early stages of making changes.

Communication is a two way thing. Communication forms the basis of any relationship and a firm basis is the foundation of a healthy relationship. Without sound footings, a relationship is unlikely to succeed to the desired degree. This criterion applies to any partnership whether it is human-to-human, animal-to-animal or human-to-animal.

Body language, and this includes facial expression, is very important for survival as well as for success in life. Although some of our body language seems to be innate, we learn more, and how to use it, from our parents, siblings and other people without ever realising we are picking it up – smiling, frowning, pointing, nodding the head, turning the head away, ignoring, waving to people from across the road, staring aggressively and so forth. We still retain this natural form of communication, both using it ourselves and reading it in others, perhaps thinking intuitively, apparently having a sixth sense even if we seldom act upon it.

However, if something doesn't feel right to you then it probably isn't.

Because our dogs lack speech as we know it, they are more in tune with our human body language than we are. In most cases, they have the time to observe us all day every day and are able to pick up on cues we are simply not aware of, so they appear to be far more intuitive than we are. On the other hand, we fill our days with so many tasks and commitments that we lack the opportunity to monitor them in the same way. Dogs operate differently to us and, because they rely on us for their survival, it makes sense for them to take notice of our ways of communicating. We are important to them in many instances, so it pays for them to be highly tuned in to what we are doing and be able to respond accordingly.

When your dog looks guilty after he has eaten the Sunday roast, it's not that he feels remorseful for his opportunist action, he is simply reacting to the stiff posture and stern expression he is looking at and relating it to the way you behaved the last time he saw that body language.

Henry looking "guilty", with closed body language

Humans 🖐

Humans use body language to communicate all the time, often without realising it.

As loving parents, long before speech arrives, we seem to understand what our baby/young child is trying to communicate, because they are so important to us. Some parents come to recognise the different cries, knowing what their children want or need before they are able to speak. How is it that many women tend to be better at knowing when their children, husband or partner are not telling the truth? They may not be able to say why they know, they just do. I feel sure that it is the subtleties of body language such as eye contact and hand gestures they are picking up on without consciously recognising all the signals they are seeing.

Just look at the frustration and anger of my teenage son as he is unable to escape me taking the photo.

Perhaps women are more practised at reading body language than men, as they are more likely to have done so when their children were young.

From my observations, many men (though not all of them) often seem to apply 'control' more than females tend to. Women, who in previous generations took the nurturing caring role in families, may be primed to notice the subtleties of body language and they also seem to make greater use of intuition. Perhaps not being able to understand the "silent" communication results in a sense of insecurity for some men and control is a way of dealing with it. That doesn't mean it's appropriate though.

Controlled relationships are unfair. Having a trusting, shared relationship would be more beneficial to both.

Isn't that what most people seek anyway?

Think about how you deal with a child. If the adult is honest and fair with them, keeping communication channels open (rather than blocking or suppressing them), they will hear far more of the child's feelings and thoughts, as well as gaining their respect, confidence and a good balanced relationship. The child will be more likely to grow in self esteem, secure in the shared relationship. If lines of communication are broken, the child will often seek other outlets which, in effect, could encourage them to be dishonest and go behind the parent's back.

Dogs

Methods of controlling dogs can be seen on television dog behaviour programmes and the restricting actions recommended can produce a similarly negative result.

On the face of it, the methods usually appear to work, but if an owner takes the same approach as the dominant parent does with their child and suppresses the dog (ignoring communication signals, whilst forcing him to be in situations he has previously been unable to cope with), there may well be repercussions such as displays of unacceptable behaviour. Alternatively, the dog may become so worried by the regime, he "shuts down", unable to react at all and lives in fear.

The dog will only be trying to find ways to cope with the situation (which he can't avoid), but what you often end up with is a behaviour which may be harder to handle than the original one the owner was trying to control.

Worse still for the dog's long term health, he may internalise his distress and risk becoming ill or developing obsessive habits such as licking and chewing himself.

This is a result of controlling another being and somewhere down the line it will have an adverse effect. Dogs with a more robust personality will cope better than others who are more sensitive, but it doesn't mean they are enjoying a good quality of life.

Dogs use their body language all the time. Comprehending it might not always come naturally to us but we can take steps to learn and understand their communication system.

Our use of speech often gets in the way of communicating with them. As I have already mentioned, dogs are far more skilled at reading our body language than we are at reading theirs. They have more experience of doing so, generally spending much of their time observing us, could we return the favour? Perhaps this suggests how committed our dogs are to us. They certainly seem to detect an alteration in our mood even before we ourselves have realised something has changed in us. Maybe dogs notice more than modern day humans because we are distracted by having too many things going on in our lives.

Living with children is quite a strain for the majority of dogs. A dog has to be aware of what the child (especially a young one) might do next. Children and dogs can to be taught to respect each other's space as well as their needs.

Dogs watch us when we have food but are very conscious of our movements all the time: they have to be, in order to feel safe and secure in their environment. We may seem as unpredictable to dogs as children can be to us.

Dogs/Humans

A good friend and colleague of mine left something important in my van. I had noticed it, but as I was seeing her the following day, decided to take it home with me. My friend phoned whilst I was out, leaving a message on the answer phone, to tell me she'd left the item behind. She hadn't asked me to call her back and, as I was busy with family commitments, I just sent a quick email to say I would bring it with me the next day. However she didn't pick up the email. In the morning, I was surprised to find my friend on my doorstep. She lived 45 minutes away from me, travelling by car, but obviously the item was important to her and being without it created considerable worry.

The point here is that even though we are of the same species, living in the age of communication, we still fail to get our message across at times, which can result in distress. My friend and I chose different forms of communication for perfectly valid reasons and we ended up with miscommunication.

Dogs face this crisis of potential misunderstanding on a daily basis, also using several forms of communication to try to get their message through.

They start with mild types of body language, progressing to the more obvious; vocalising by barking, whining and growling before finally resorting to using their teeth. Usually biting gets the dog noticed! The consequence for many a dog is being put to sleep, simply because it hasn't been understood. The dog's death in these cases is down to our ignorance.

How frustrating and distressing for them is our failure to get the message, day in, day out? These ongoing pressures have the potential to cause some serious health issues if not dealt with. Can you think how you might feel and the behaviours you might adopt if you were constantly ignored? How desperate might you become? Well, how easily do we become angry? If I were a dog, I think I might resort to biting or certainly have some kind of behavioural problem if I had to endure being misunderstood and disregarded day after day.

So many forms of contact, yet we can still miscommunicate with one another even when we speak the same language.

In this wedding photo there are several forms of communication taking place: body language (from everyone), speech, eye contact and touch.

Communicating a need may be shown in various ways.

Chewing choices

One area that constantly gets wires crossed is damage caused when a dog is left unsupervised.

> *Chewing is a natural behaviour for a dog. Many dogs need to chew to help relieve stress.*

If owners understand this fact, they can approach the issue more positively. Regularly coming home to scenes of destruction means there is a need to discover whether the dog is simply enjoying the process of chewing or if there is an underlying problem about being left. In the first scenario, simply being given opportunities to chew when there is a need may reduce damage to inappropriate items when they are alone. You need to know the dog in question. For example, chewing options may create frustration and high arousal for some dogs, which will be clearly seen in the way they respond when given them but, for many, being provided with appropriate opportunities to chew will help enormously. The chewing action releases endorphins which will help the dog feel more relaxed, but the items provided must be suitable for them.

Jaffa has a chewing choice, variety is the spice of life.

Dogs enjoy different textures. This may vary during the day and from day to day and dog to dog.

We may not always recognise when a dog has the urge to chew. For example some dogs will want to chew just after they've eaten, others when visitors are at the house (even perhaps when members of the family come home), out in the park, after a walk, maybe when we sit down to relax and so on. The way a dog chews is significant. If he quietly lies down, and calmly gets on with it, that's fine but some may gnaw away with such intensity that it's almost an obsession and that suggests they may be feeling pressure.

Other dogs may become wound up by what and how they chew. Even the time of day and perhaps how tired they are is relevant for a few dogs and their emotional state could well be a factor. For the dog to be comfortable, a relaxed, calm environment is required along with a degree of privacy and all dogs need fair and appropriate boundaries in place so that their security can be guaranteed; e.g. door / gate closed if other dogs / people are around.

If damage is being caused because the dog is not coping when left, then teaching him to be alone is the first thing to work on. This is a gradual process of building up his capacity to cope without familiar people around and it begins with him being on his own but with his owner in view although not directly available to him. Having items to chew on at these times may help with the emotional side as he learns to deal with being apart from the owner. Ideally it's preferable that he's not left while this teaching is taking place but if, occasionally, he must be alone for very short times, it may be appropriate to leave him with one or two known items that are safe for him, which ensures he can relieve some frustration if necessary. But does this make the situation better or worse? The answer will depend on the individual.

Preventing chewing of inappropriate items can be challenging but, with a bit of thought and understanding, it's possible to work out a suitable programme of chewing for your own dog. There are dogs who can benefit from chewing for a short time in a relaxed manner but, if it goes on for too long, they may start to become worried, animated and / or frustrated. Before this happens, gently and nonchalantly changing the situation can lead to a positive finish to the activity and in time the dog learns to develop self-control. In some cases, the activity of chewing itself may present problems for a dog; perhaps he has negative associations for whatever reason or, indeed, been deprived of it in the past resulting in an over-the-top reaction when opportunities do arise. Having access to suitable chewing options is important for a dog and monitoring him to note when he is communicating this need to chew is our responsibility. Observe what is happening in his environment and try to work out if there is a reason why he needs to chew and perhaps you can investigate further.

For dogs who have demonstrated that they can deal with chewing sensibly and derive benefit from it, safe options can be left freely available, as we cannot know exactly when the dog may need to chew.

Some dogs prefer softer textures; such as safe soft toys and cardboard, whereas others might prefer wooden or harder resources.

These chewing items need to be checked for safety and renewed every now and then. Dogs can become too familiar with the same things left lying around.

24

Dogs 🐾

When we have dogs we have a great opportunity to spend time observing them, how they communicate with each other and us, using their non-verbal language.

For instance, if your dog sees another dog but chooses not to interact with it, he may turn his head away. Should the newcomer ignore this communication and persist in approaching, your dog may then turn his back on the other dog (looking right away) and moving very slowly. Your dog may sit down, then turn around and lie down. Finally, if the previous strategy hasn't worked, he may get up and walk slowly away.

All this happens very quickly, so it is easy to miss, indeed most of us do miss it until we become experienced and practised in observing dogs.

Situations can rapidly get out of hand when excitement becomes too much, as can be seen when children are left to play unsupervised, it often "all ends in tears". A dog experiencing another dog in an over excited state may try communication to begin with. For example, he may begin to yawn, making the yawns more exaggerated before moving away very slowly in an attempt to calm down the other dog, but if the communication doesn't work, the first dog may also start to get "silly" and show displacement behaviour (explained later) because he doesn't know what else to do.

If a dog is over-excited he has the potential to become dangerous. Fur may fly.

We can emulate some of the dog's body language with simple movements such as turning our head away from unwanted behaviour, indicating that we don't support their actions but remain available to an approach and are not excluding them. We can also back off, moving slowly and calmly (remembering to avert our gaze), speaking softly if needed.

If you feel tension is rising in the dog, usually just being placid and carrying on with whatever you are doing in a quiet way, perhaps saying very little, is likely to be an advantage, benefitting both the dog and you, providing that's not totally alien to him. As is often the case, much depends on the dog and various influencing factors.

If we feel angry, it's probably best not to speak at all because the emotion may well come across in the voice and make matters worse. In general, I tend to keep fairly quiet when with my dogs; I find it calming but, if anything does need saying, I keep the tone soft and relaxed, which in turn helps to take away any frustration, leaving empathy and understanding for the dog. This approach, more often than not, has a positive effect when challenging situations arise. Handling matters in this gentle way lowers the emotional temperature and gives space for clearer thought and observation. Just remember to breathe! Dogs certainly pick up on our rate of breathing and, when it stops, they know something is different and, perhaps, requires a response from them.

In everyday actions your dog may wonder whether it involves him, so casually letting him know what you are doing or going to do seems to help some. Keeping it short such as "I'm going upstairs to fetch something" or perhaps "I'll be back soon" includes the dog in our daily lives in a nonchalant way and sounds softer than a "stay" instruction. When this is done regularly, dogs get to understand what is happening and know that nothing is expected of them in this instance.

When unwanted behaviour occurs, if you have chance, think rather than react immediately. Once all has calmed down, take the chance to reflect on what just took place and consider what could be changed another time to improve the outcome. Think about the environment the dog is in, the situation, who is there and what is going on – sights, sounds, smells / taste and touch too. What has been happening beforehand? How long has the dog been in the situation that prompted the reaction and how often does it happen? Just ignoring behaviour may work with some dogs some of the time but bear in mind how it feels to be ignored repeatedly with no option to interact or to learn from the situation. Consider the negative impact your actions may have on your dog. Being ignored seems so final - closure with no chance to re-open communication. Changing your body language to give the dog or person a chance to remain connected to you will pay off in the end.

Think about why the dog is using unwanted behaviour? What is unwanted behaviour anyway? Who decides what is acceptable and what isn't? What you may not like, may be perfectly all right in a different household. What is the dog saying when he behaves in this way? Maybe he's trying to tell you that he's not at ease and needs something to be changed. It is a good idea to look at the various components that make the dog's behaviour "unwanted". Sometimes it seems that we focus most of our attention on what we don't want from a dog - "stop that, leave it alone, no, don't do that, what's wrong with you?" Perhaps, when he's done something we are not happy about, we are looking at and touching the dog, which draws greater attention to the behaviour we don't want and may, inadvertently, encourage the very thing we are trying to stop. Shouting at, getting angry or physically restraining the dog may appear to work temporarily, but he certainly doesn't grasp what it all means or what we want from him. His response will be coming from a place of fear thus depriving him of the opportunity to learn what we want him to do instead. Yes, he knows his owner is angry, but a far more effective way of ending unwanted behaviour is to use body language because this is what the dog understands.

What else can we do? How about preventing some of the situations that trigger the dog before he has the need to misbehave? Look to see what the dog is finding stressful and try to help him out by waiting calmly until he indicates he is ready to be moved away and is willing to go with you. Where you can, reduce exposure to what prompts him to react. Being understanding and gentle will help him and retain a positive relationship.

Of course persistency and consistency in all your dealings with the dog must still come into the equation, however, good use of body language will defuse matters and help calm things down.

Be aware that for a dog, lengthy sentences and continual chatter are incomprehensible and teaches very little. Some dogs find our constant talking quite distracting. In addition, most dogs are sensitive to the emotion in our voices and that influences their behaviour as a consequence.

Our attitude and the tone we use when speaking to dogs gives them clearer information than the actual words do but body language "speaks" to them most naturally. Many dogs will be quite comfortable with us mimicking their simplest communication signals and respond very well.

In my experience, it has amazing results with most breeds, indeed with other species too.

However, I have also seen some dogs become worried by our attempts at copying certain forms of their body language. As with everything else, it depends on the individual, the situation, and also the way in which it is done. If the person trying to copy the dog's body language is highly stressed themselves, then it is not likely to work.

Some dogs need to get used to the idea of humans acting out their language and they may need a few repetitions before they realise their owner is actually "speaking" to them. The more people practise using body language, the better they get at it.

A dog attracts another when one shows interest in a particular smell or item. We can use their curiosity to our advantage occasionally if they need help because they don't have the necessary skills to solve a particular problem. If a person interacts with something, most dogs will come to investigate, especially when our full attention is on it. Care needs to be taken to use this sparingly. Dogs know if it's genuine, so being honest is essential. Dogs are more likely to trust when it's genuine, just as we are. Tricking them leads to a lack of trust. The Border Collie (Bobby) is blind, yet is still able to use good body language and communication skills.
(Thanks to Carol Ilic for permission to use this photo of Bobby)

Dogs, like people, are inquisitive so be careful if you don't want to draw their attention to what you are doing. On the other hand if you want to reinforce a behaviour, giving your attention may well achieve it.

Communication in practice

These two photos show how easy and effective it can be when using the dog's own communication system. It works without us becoming angry or having to constantly repeat commands.

In the first photo, Hagrid invades my granddaughter's space. Calmly, slowly she turns away from him. He instantly understands and also turns and walks away. This works for Hagrid and my granddaughter but for some dogs, further communication such as moving slowly away from them, might be called for. It will vary from dog to dog and person to person, depending on previous experiences and other factors. Whatever is necessary, it's more effective if all actions are carried out slowly and calmly without commanding the dog. After all, dogs do it without any excitement and noise so why not us?

I think this is a wonderful interaction as neither makes a fuss. There simply isn't any need for commands (which the dogs don't always understand). Usually they are reacting to the pitch of our voice and tense body language. All dogs use the same communication system to understand each other. If we are prepared to learn their language, as above, we will be better able to "speak" with and respond to dogs.

My granddaughter was scared of dogs but has learnt how to understand them and communicate with them by using body language.

Humans

There are many factors which can influence the way we communicate. Consider the use of language. The word "command" is a good example. Think about your own feelings if someone commands you to do something. What expectations does it create? Do you have a choice? Do you feel threatened or under pressure? What would happen if you didn't obey? Now think again: what does it feel like when someone gives you an encouraging signal instead or makes a suggestion?

In addition, the specific words used may subtly influence thought processes and actions so potentially can have an impact on the relationship you have with your dog.

If we would like a calm and balanced dog, we must first learn to be calm and balanced ourselves. In addition, a relaxed dog is in a better position to understand us. The same principle applies as with children, both learn from our example.

Have you noticed people who wish to avoid attention from dogs stay quiet, making no effort to interact? A well balanced dog very often goes over to those who are largely unresponsive to their advances, seeming to prefer being with them rather than the people trying to "pet, fuss or love" him, often in an excited manner. The dog is in effect communicating to us his preferred human demeanour. Our efforts to interact with dogs will be far more successful and productive if we use body language, making small movements in a subtle, natural way.

Dogs/Humans

Just like us, dogs want a peaceful life. They are not naturally aggressive. Aggression is usually displayed because other, more subtle signs have gone by without being noticed. In most cases, it is the act of a fearful or frustrated dog who has learned to use this behaviour because his normal communication signals (body language) have been missed or even punished. When dogs growl, bare their teeth, lunge, bark, or use ignoring signals, they are far too often viewed as defiant or (using that outdated term) "dominant", and are then punished for their "bad" behaviour.

If we choose to back off, it's okay because we are showing that we recognise the dog is under pressure of some sort. It means we're prepared to be open to them and respect their communication.

Continuing the analogy of parents and children, if we keep telling a child not to misbehave and we are constantly ignored, how often will our own behaviour escalate to aggression; shouting at them, or even smacking them? In such circumstances, isn't it understandable, if not acceptable, for us to lose our temper? Isn't it also understandable for a dog to become frustrated and lose control? Both species can become aggressive if not listened to.

I have learned this: if my dogs growl or curl their lip, it is a good sign, because, even though they are really struggling, they know it is safe to tell me and are confident that they will be acknowledged appropriately. I will back off, doing whatever is necessary to defuse the situation, helping them out so they have no need to escalate to further aggressive behaviour.

None of the strong (high arousal) communication signals should be copied by humans, as the outcome is potentially dangerous.

Key points | The basis of shared relationships

 No controlled relationship is fair. Wouldn't it be less stressful for both partners to have a trusting shared relationship instead?

 Dogs use their body language all the time. Becoming more aware of it means we can learn and understand their communication system but that requires us to make an effort.

 If we would like a calm and balanced dog, we must first learn to be calm and balanced ourselves. In addition, a relaxed dog is in a better position to understand us. The same principle applies as with children, both learn from our example.

 For dogs, much of our chatter means and teaches him little but they pick up on the emotion in our voices and respond accordingly. Take time to consider how the words you choose make you feel and can affect how you react. Our words influence our body language.

Bullying

Improving observational skills enables us to pick up subtle body language signals dogs use when bullying, giving us the opportunity to intervene appropriately.

Dogs 🐾

My 13-stone (83 Kg) rescued male English Mastiff employed bullying behaviour on the humans in my house when I first had him. He was worried, due mainly to his past experiences and didn't feel safe or secure in this new environment. When a dog feels sure of his surroundings, there is no need for him to use such behaviours.

Bullying is a way a dog communicates his insecurity in a situation and can take the form of guarding space, a person, another dog, in fact anything that is of importance to him. You also may see barging into an animal / person, nipping, invading another's space, stalking, dive-bombing (whether that is actual contact or near misses, either way it might be intimidating to the receiver), barking or growling, mounting, standing over, nagging people / animals to play and not responding to their evasive communication, stealing items then flaunting them in front of the "robbed" individual and other similar actions. Just like people who use certain behaviours when they are fearful, unwell, vulnerable or feel threatened in some way, or simply haven't learnt an appropriate way to behave, dogs can do too. We understand that they are not doing this because they want to; there are emotions actually driving the behaviour.

If we begin to appreciate that the dog is not acting maliciously but that he has a problem either with something in his daily routine or what we might be doing with him, it might help us to be more sympathetic. It is his way of communicating that something is frightening, making him feel unsafe. The dog needs help to rectify the situation. By being there, consistently, for the dog, offering understanding, support and guidance towards other options, working on building confidence as well as using boundaries and barriers, the behaviours are likely to disappear, once he can trust enough to feel safe. Punishment, demands and commands will make matters worse and the behaviour has the potential to become more severe too, so it's really worth addressing. Often we see bullying when dogs have too much or too little freedom and / or inconsistencies in their management. Some may have experienced the behaviours mentioned from other animals or people, so learn to repeat the process themselves.

By working with Hagrid, helping him to feel secure, supported and loved, for the most part, he stopped using these tactics to control my family and myself. I find it interesting to note that he sometimes reverts back to old behaviours when he is feeling more vulnerable; he is a dog who daily has to manage many health issues, which cause him to be less aware of his surroundings, so some days may feel worse than on others. Boundaries are in place to protect him and the rest of us so he doesn't need to exhibit those behaviours but, like all humans, we sometimes make errors and things don't always go as planned and, on occasions, the unexpected happens and we just have to do the best we can at the time with the available resources. We also have to accept that some dogs do have problems; like humans no one is perfect. However, it's up to us to remain flexible and put whatever is required in place to make life as pleasant and as comfortable as possible. If Hagrid started to bully more and more, we would need to review what we were doing. That's how it works.

Hagrid growled at me in the early days but I respected his communication. I set boundaries in place and, because my family and I have been consistent in applying them, he understands what he can do and what isn't allowed.

Much of this is done through the use of body language with little verbal language involved. I never tell my dogs off, as this teaches the dogs nothing about the message behind our words; they just know we're angry with them and this has a negative influence on our relationship with them, as it does with any relationship.

Having previously ignored unwanted actions, I have now learned to work with behaviour I don't want or like; by using techniques appropriate for different situations and that will vary depending on what is taking place, the intensity of the behaviour, how often it happens and how long it goes on for. Dogs use their communication to do just that – communicate; so even if we don't like what we see, they are telling us something and we need to listen and respond in a way that will help the dog. They don't act to spite us. Why not simply accept the dog is behaving in that way because something bothers him, just as a baby cries when he needs your help? There will be a valid reason behind the dog's actions. You just need to work it out!

Hagrid has learned that nothing bad is going to happen to him and, indeed, nothing bad has happened to him since he's been with us. We respect each other. By working in this way, Hagrid has stopped trying to control my family and myself.

I am using this picture of Hagrid with my granddaughter as it shows what his bullying behaviour used to look like when he approached my son from behind and nipped him. Coming from behind is a common tactic for a bully. In this instance however, he was simply showing interest. It's important, when observing behaviour not to jump to conclusions based on just one aspect of what the dog is doing, but to watch for a period of time and reach a measured conclusion based on all the evidence. (Go to page 108).

Dominance reduction methods (control) had already been used on Hagrid and I am sure this is why he exhibited bullying behaviour particularly with my adolescent son.

Hagrid used to stalk my son, trying to bite him from behind when he moved, or even if he moved his hands.

The actions I took based on the contents of this book are the complete opposite of what many behaviour specialists might recommend, but the result is the best relationship I have ever had with any dog I have cared for, with no further bullying to anyone else.

In fact, I now truly care for my dogs and realise that a few years back I was dominating Jaffa through my ignorance of her needs. She was a dog who didn't dare react to anything and became ill mainly due to this repression. She suffered from various ailments, among them colitis, which was quite severe. However, she no longer experiences this unpleasant complaint, largely due to my having learned to understand her signals. At first, Jaffa had given up trying to use her communication (shut down) as, from her point of view, it wasn't working.

Allowing Jaffa to explore, where as (previously I would have told her off for this), I now remove items I don't want her to have and give her some freedom to make decisions and build confidence. As well as this, her health improved drastically.

I took no notice of what she was saying to me, simply forcing my regime on her. It is possible to teach a dog to communicate again by respecting his wishes, giving him choices, stopping all the controlling commands such as sit, down, heel, as well as forcing him to be around dogs in an attempt to "socialise" him and so on. We learnt to enjoy each other's company, having a good time together.

Jaffa developed a brilliant recall as she wanted to be with me. In addition, her health improved, with her colitis disappearing for many years.

Prior to this, she would run away regularly. I worked on developing a good relationship with her whilst using the prevention and management skills I had learned. It has probably been harder to work with my Cavalier as I was the one who had employed the dominance rules on her in the first place, so it took some time before she felt she could trust me.

Bullying can often be very subtle; people rarely notice the communication that goes on between dogs living together. The Mastiff (Kaos) manipulated Jaffa regularly. She controlled space by giving Jaffa "one of those looks". Kaos also restricted Jaffa's access to the water bowl and other resources. Some dogs find it uncomfortable to eat and drink in close proximity to a controlling dog. Well I would feel uneasy too if it were me.

I am convinced that Kaos became a bully due to my over use of commands as well as bad training experiences and excessive play as a puppy with no boundaries in place.

Key points | Bullying

 It is important to observe your dog's behaviour in several situations before reaching a conclusion based on all the evidence.

 A dog or person will use pushy behaviour when he is insecure and doesn't feel safe.

 Use of non-confrontational methods enables us to have a mutually respectful relationship.

 Dominance based training can cause a dog to exhibit bullying behaviour; it's what he's been trained to understand.

The need for body language

Body language is vital for communication and survival. We may not always be aware when using it, but dogs certainly are. Our body language creates the need for the dog to respond.

Dogs/Humans 🐾 ✋

Dogs have a variety of signals they use to indicate to others how they are feeling and their intentions.

We also have signals we use to indicate to others how we are feeling, regardless of what we may be saying. We smile to show we are a happy and pleasant person, reassuring others we mean no harm. We can also smile nervously when faced with someone we are not too sure of, perhaps persuading them to do the same or as appeasement. Maybe we fold our arms and cross our legs to indicate we are not happy with what someone has said, as a form of protecting ourselves, as a block. We may feel vulnerable. The situation or context in which this happens must be taken into consideration though. Crossing their arms and legs could simply mean the person is cold and wants to go to the toilet!

All dogs will have certain signals they use most readily. One of my dogs often sneezes again and again as she becomes excited. Another yawns quite a lot. When he doesn't know what to do or is uncomfortable, he scratches himself, often accompanied by a yawn. Adult humans will sometimes tease children; the youngster might try to avoid being the focus of everyone's attention by hiding their face, wriggling around or burying their head in a cushion, not knowing what to do to avoid the adults' gazes and laughter.

Some dogs also become "silly", wriggling around in a similar way. Many Golden Retrievers tend to scratch when they feel a little uneasy or overwhelmed. I am not saying they feel embarrassed as such, but it is a sign of discomfort with what is happening to them at the time.

Dogs of the same breed often favour the same signals. I have also seen a number of dogs who will copy another dog, responding with a matching signal. Black dogs seem to use the tongue or mouth to communicate, such as lip licks and yawns. Perhaps these show up better against the background of black fur which tends to make other facial signals less easy to read.

As different breeds tend to depend on similar signs so do people from different cultures. Family members share similar mannerisms even if they've been separated at birth. We have ways of coping with uncomfortable situations. For instance some may stroke their necks, put their fingers in their mouth, twist their hair, whilst others may mirror body language or pretend they are looking at something else. Well, dogs do it too. Simply put, dogs make extensive use of body language to "talk" to each other.

People have the option to walk away from situations they don't like; dogs rarely do, so they use body language instead to maintain a calm atmosphere.

Once educated to the subtleties of dogs' body language, it becomes obvious when two well adjusted adult dogs meet, a conversation is actually taking place. Often you see them mirroring one another's body shape and stance to ensure a peaceful encounter.

These dogs know and like each other. They meet calmly in a polite way, curving their bodies, their tails wagging at the same height, ears relaxed, in a similar stance, mirroring one another. A head-on approach would be impolite between dogs who are strangers. This is less of a problem for dogs who are familiar with each other.

43

An ideal meeting between two dogs

1. Dog A is strolling along sniffing here and there when he catches sight of an approaching dog in the distance.

2. Immediately, dog A averts his eyes, pretending to look in another direction. Polite well adjusted dogs will avoid staring because it can seem intrusive.

3. At this point, if he chooses, dog A may be far enough away from dog B to exit the situation by heading in a different direction and that is the end of the matter.

4. Let's say the dogs continue towards one another; now dog B has spotted dog A, and he performs the same "look away" gesture.

5. They are off to a good start. This is polite body language, indicating neither dog is confrontational at the moment.

6. As the two move closer, both slow down a little, still glancing briefly at each other then looking away. Dog A may pretend he's seen something in the distance and appears to be concentrating on this.

7. As they draw closer still, dog B may sniff at the ground whilst checking to make sure the approaching dog is still not a danger to him. As the distance between them gets smaller, they may progress to some alternate sniffing of the environment; one puts his nose down, scanning at the same time, but also giving the other the opportunity to move closer.

8. During the approach they may exchange some facial gestures. These may include lip-licks or narrowing of the eyes, before progressing to a head dip, turning the head or body away, tails held in a fairly relaxed manner.

9. Towards the end of the meeting, both dogs may curve around one another, avoiding the head-on approach which could appear to be threatening, as well as enabling them not to exchange full eye contact. This can end with the two dogs sniffing each other at both ends.

10. After passing, one or both dogs may look back and give a shake, which they often do, perhaps to relieve the tension of an encounter.

A typical meeting between two calm and well-adjusted adult dogs:

1   2

Whilst out on a walk Jaffa, and I came across a dog without an owner. It was a fairly polite meeting although Jaffa did think the sniffing of her bottom was a little too intrusive.

1. *The first two photos show the white dog approaching whilst Jaffa's body is in a curve.*
2. *They skirt around each other; the white dog curves then sniffs Jaffa.*
3. *Jaffa becomes uncomfortable and appears to have seen something in the distance.*

4 5

She turns to look intently at him. He responds by turning his head and body away from her.

She curves again as he walks off.

Lovely body language from both dogs.

Some dogs resort to aggressive behaviour when they meet on taut leads and tight restraint can create a tense situation. However, depending on their skills and experience, a slack lead could lead to either or both dogs feeling disconnected by the lack of support from the handler and would benefit from light tension on the long line. Appropriate handling and a positive relationship with the dog make such a difference to the outcome of an encounter.

Humans meeting

Compare the dogs' actions to what happens when two people meet whilst out on a walk in the countryside:

1. You are on your own, appreciating the beautiful countryside, deep in your thoughts, when you look up and see a person heading in your direction. If you are a woman and it is a male approaching, this could be interpreted as a potentially dangerous situation.

2. No-one else is around. You are immediately brought out of your tranquil state and may well pretend that you've not seen the other person yet by taking great interest in your surroundings as a cover up. This may offer you a little confidence and avoid the slight embarrassment of staring at a stranger.

3. If the opportunity is there, you may take an escape route and go another way. However, let's say you carry on.

4. Okay, you've seen each other, there's no avoiding it now.

5. You put your hands in your pockets as you come closer. You both avert your eyes and whilst still looking away you check your watch (not registering the time though).

6. He looks the other way too, avoiding a confrontational stare. Safe so far!

7. He may start to play with his (wait for it!) – mobile phone.

8. You may adjust your clothing, fiddle with keys and other items in your pocket, scratch your neck, just nervously fidgeting around.

9. The other person can see you are no threat, you mean no harm. Hopefully, they reciprocate and you can continue on your path.

10. People often mirror each other's body language too, you curve around him to make more space as you pass, or vice versa, or perhaps you both step a little to the side.

11. You both have fairly relaxed faces, maybe exchanging a false smile (not using eyes) or mutter a greeting, whilst briefly glancing at each other.

12. When you have passed, perhaps you look round from a safe distance.

13. He may do likewise, which is embarrassing if you do it at the same time!

The adult and child mirror each others' body language.

This is how children learn about life and how to do things. Children are great at mimicking adults, learning things whether they are intended for them or not.

Not so different are we?

Humans and dogs are not so different are they but how aware are we of what we are actually doing? Frequently we carry out actions without consciously noticing or thinking about them. What we can do is recognise that our dogs experience similar emotions to us and we need to give off appropriate body signals for their situation. Unless we make necessary adjustments to accommodate them, they may be unable to communicate effectively. When dogs are taken into situations they'd rather avoid, they often find it hard to behave as their instincts prompt them to, particularly if they are restricted by short, tight leads.

It's unnatural for dogs to approach head-on; they prefer to give each other space by curving around but there just isn't the room for this on most pavements and footpaths. Yet, this is what they are so often expected to do.

Now let's have a look at what humans do when they meet a dog coming toward them, with or without an owner:

Very often we will walk head on towards dog and owner, having full eye contact with the dog. Humans rarely greet strangers in such an informal way. How might we feel if a stranger did this to us? Such actions can be quite threatening for a dog. We can make it much easier for them if we think about how we approach – slow down, curve around them, have indirect eye contact and resist the temptation to touch unfamiliar dogs.

Key points | The need for body language

 Dogs have a variety of signals they use to indicate to others how they are feeling and their intentions.

 Every dog is different and will use their own combination of preferred body language signals.

 People have the choice to walk away from situations they don't like; dogs rarely have the option to do this, so they use body language to maintain calm. They need to be given the space and freedom to do so. Using a long line can give the dog the opportunity to be able to do this more easily.

 It is unnatural for dogs to approach head-on; they prefer to give each other space by curving around but there isn't room for this on most pavements and footpaths.

Simple changes, big impact

I had been warned that the young reindeers would not approach any people, but simple changes to my body language made all the difference. The onlooking zoo staff were amazed when the reindeer chose to come close.

By learning and understanding what dogs are trying to communicate in various situations we are able to recognise the impact we have on them. Once we accept this, we are in a position to change things, making life easier for our own dogs as well as others we meet. We are less threatening to most animals if we change our body language appropriately in response to theirs.

Understanding the dog by putting ourselves in their position is the best thing we can do for them in the early stages of making changes.

I am proposing that we use some "dog friendly" manners such as resisting the temptation to reach our hands out and touch them the moment we get close, avoiding direct eye contact and taking care how we speak to them, keeping our voices soft and quiet.

If they feel comfortable they will come and sniff you, so, just allow them to do this in their own time and then move away politely. Some dogs, providing they are not especially sound sensitive, may tolerate you talking quietly and gently to them (but not *at* them). We don't have to stroke all dogs at the first opportunity. It is hard to deny ourselves this pleasure but we can do it if we try. When someone reaches their hand out to a dog, you often see him back off, lowering his head to avoid the outstretched hand and turning away, yawning or giving another low level communication signal, perhaps making some attempt to leave the vicinity.

On the other hand, the dog may respond by becoming wriggly and over excited, and may possibly jump up. Some people may tell him off whilst others encourage it. How confusing must that be for the dog?

The bouncy response doesn't mean he enjoys human touch, it is usually a coping strategy where the dog is indicating that, actually, he is worried by the human.

Dogs rarely touch one another unless they know each other very well. In their terms, touch can be a form of confrontation, conflict, or a sexual approach. When they sniff another dog, it is a different form of making contact, usually achieved by nose to rear end, in a non invasive, "fact finding" manner and providing it doesn't go on too long, is generally regarded as an acceptable form of address between dogs.

Humans tend to be more tactile than dogs and certainly use touch in a different way. We also generally understand the intention behind varying types of touch. Unless someone is very familiar to the dog, it's best that we limit physical contact with him and keep touch for our own kind.

Many children like to be cuddled by familiar adults, but strangers are a totally different matter, for children and adults as well.

What would the parents' responses be if strangers were to walk up to their children daring to touch them? Have you tried ruffling up someone's hair when they are concentrating on something? How do they react? This often happens to dogs. Can you see how tolerant dogs really are? I am sorry to say we humans invade dogs' space far too often. Once this is realised though, we can be aware of our impact on all the dogs we encounter and treat them more respectfully.

Boys enjoying time at a country fete. Somehow I don't think the boys or their parents would take kindly to strangers approaching, patting them on the head, stroking them or staring. (In fact, don't we tell our children not to stare?) If people they don't know come up and touch them, children may start to react, perhaps running away or protesting. They may develop a fear of strangers, as many dogs do, for the same reasons.

Most dogs, depending on previous experiences, may become accustomed to their owners touching or holding them (not that they necessarily like it), but it is not fair to expect any dog to endure this behaviour from anyone else, so perhaps try to protect your dog and educate other people. Some dogs may like being stroked, but the majority of people are unable to detect the differences between a dog showing signs of enjoyment, tolerance (feeling he has no option other than to endure being stroked) or insecurity.

This is why it is of paramount importance that everyone who comes into contact with dogs is aware of how they communicate and what they are telling us; only then do we stand a chance of knowing whether it is appropriate to touch them or not and we need to carry on monitoring their communication throughout the interaction.

Touch is important; a basic need for survival and can be a wonderful experience, enhancing life, easing pain and discomfort. However, I know only too well what it is like to have requests not to touch my dogs ignored. Being touched when both parties are in agreement is great, so if a dog indicates he is ready to be stroked or handled in some way that's fine, but we need to be sure that we are not unintentionally exploiting their cooperative nature to satisfy our wish to make contact with them. We touch dogs for different reasons - because we like them and it makes us feel good; because the dog requests interaction with us; it's something for us to do and focus on; because some dogs need grooming and are unable to do this for themselves; displacement activity - an outlet for our internal feelings - perhaps when chatting to someone in the street, on the phone: nervously patting / fussing the dog while at the vets and there will be others too.

Just looking at or talking to a dog or person is making contact and can be a pleasant or unpleasant encounter for either.

Being touched against your wishes can have negative consequences and may have long term effects depending on how touch is applied, how the person / animal experiences it and how often that situation arises, but without consent the action is likely to be intrusive. A dog is able to say if he likes to be touched but only if he's been given the opportunity to do so. It's something for them to learn. What usually happens is that, for example, out on a walk (or in their own home) people who may well be complete strangers come up and stroke the dog and the owners, liking the attention shown to their dog, encourage it. The dog then comes to expect this to happen with everyone they meet and often become 'wiggly' and jump up in anticipation or perhaps anxiety. The wiggly, jumping up behaviour is not always acceptable to everyone so the dog could well be told off and made to get down. Some dogs may become still when approached and touched. Such a dog is likely to be seen as a well behaved but, in reality, he may well be quite concerned and just doing what he can to cope with a stranger making contact. Either way, humans have created uncertainty in the dog's mind and his actions are probably a result of this; the static situation and the focus on him only adds to the pressure. It will be harder for the animal to cope if he is in areas that offer little or no opportunity to use the environment as a distraction as he deals with the intrusive human behaviour.

Licking the person who is touching them, rolling onto their backs, becoming animated and excited, chewing the lead, pushing / leaning against a person are some other displacement behaviours that can easily be misinterpreted as a dog wanting to be handled. Children also react in a 'silly, excitable' way when attention is on them – showing off. They might also cling to their parent or adult they feel secure with. It doesn't always mean that they like being in the spotlight; it's more likely due to discomfort and embarrassment.

Some rescue dogs have issues with being touched because of broken relationships, loss of trust, rough handling and bad treatment. Then there are dogs who will have had little or only negative experience of human contact, coming from puppy mills / farms, laboratories, even some from private homes can be victims of minimal, poor human touch or perhaps none at all. In extreme cases, our friendly attempt to reach out to them may be met with the dog saying very firmly "Hands off!" using teeth and vocalising but with kindness, compassion and sensitivity, heeding their communication, they can overcome their negative experiences. By waiting until a dog shows he is comfortable with being approached and remaining totally relaxed for a while before you even attempt to make contact, you help him slowly build / rebuild trust but this cannot be rushed. It takes time (some dogs may need weeks, months or longer) and patience, always working on their terms, but they can learn to trust again and that is incredibly rewarding for dog and human.

1. Spending time with your dog, having a shared relationship and using relaxed, open body language reduces the need to ask (or tell) them to do things. Being reasonably close and side on to the dog, at the same time respecting their personal space, encourages the dog to want to be with you.

2. Here Hagrid turns in my direction, without the need for me to tell him. Put simply, a long line applied correctly as a boundary, time, patience, mutual respect, a good relationship and inviting body language and you have the tools needed for this natural way of working with dogs.

3. By staying close to Hagrid, with light tension on the lead (maintained by him) he is able to sense in which direction we are going. Being patient and applying my knowledge of this way of working with dogs, I'm able to give Hagrid the time he requires to digest and process the information then come with me voluntarily, when he is ready. As he sniffs I wait for him. A long line gives you a connection with your dog and is a valuable tool that helps to build trust and confidence.

4. Hagrid and I move along together, choosing to be with one another. When Hagrid came to me 2 years before these photos were taken he didn't trust people. He pulled, always at the end of an 8 metre line, never looking round to connect with the person at the other end. A long line offers reassurance to the dog and is a positive, necessary tool, which helps the dog to feel secure in knowing the owner is close by. It also plays a part in developing the relationship between dog and owner, providing the person respects communication signals given by the dog. Off lead dogs are susceptible to unwanted approaches from other dogs, can chase wildlife, have opportunities to learn how to bully or are vulnerable to being bullied themselves, which undermines confidence. If a long line is used, you remove potential negative pressure from the dog / owner relationship which an unreliable recall can cause. At appropriate times and places, being off lead is good for a dog but, even if the handler is fluent at identifying canine communication, being at a distance makes it difficult to spot what is going on with dog-to-dog meetings and to respond effectively to potential problems.

First impressions

This sequence of pictures indicates how our actions affect dogs:

My hand is on Hagrid's chest. He is fairly comfortable with this and his body leaning into me. His mouth is relaxed.

As I move my hand to touch his ear he becomes uncomfortable and leans his body slightly away from me whilst turning his head. His mouth closes.

I continue to reach towards his ear. He transfers his weight to his other side, moving further away from me, lifting a paw slightly, ears drawn back and jaw tense as he keeps an eye on me, indicating how unhappy he is with what my hands are doing.

As I return my hand to his chest his weight begins to turn into my body again, his head comes closer to mine, although his mouth remains closed. He looks right into my face so I respond by giving him a soft expression, close my eyes a little (careful not to intently look at him, which is threatening for dogs) and tilt my head slightly away therefore making the situation easier.

This was the first time I had met Hagrid, so examining his ear was quite intrusive for him. He was responsive to where my hands were and what they were doing.

Key points | Simple changes, big impact

 Understanding the dog by putting ourselves into their position is the best thing we can do for them in the early stages of making changes.

 Most humans are likely to be more tactile than the majority of dogs and certainly use direct contact in a different way. Unless being offered by someone very familiar to the dog, it's best that we keep touch for our own kind.

Why not educate those who are less well known to the dog in how to act respectfully toward them by avoiding direct eye contact, touch and verbal communication?

 A bouncy response doesn't mean the dog enjoys human touch, it is usually a coping strategy where the dog is indicating that, actually, he is worried by the human.

Canine communication signals

Dogs communicate their intentions to one another. The adult dog curves, tail high, head down and turned away (so no direct eye contact). The youngster offers a play bow, his tail raised and wagging, to the older dog.

Dogs 🐾

Low level/mild signals:

dogs also use these signals to communicate with other species and, on a number of occasions, I have witnessed other animals using the same kind of signals.

- Lip licking
- Paw lift
- Head turn
- Ignoring
- Lowered tail
- Narrowing of eyes
- Whining*
- Looking away
- Blinking
- Sniffing the ground
- Head dip
- Yawning
- Sneezing
- Shake off (when he shakes but is not wet, as we might stretch or breathe out after a close encounter or slightly scary moment.)

Stronger signals:

a dog who is becoming anxious, making his feelings known more clearly:

- Turning body away
- Lying down
- Sitting down
- Freezing
- Tail between legs
- Growling*
- Baring teeth
- Lunging
- Lunging and barking*
- Lowered body
- Body tension
- Sweaty paws
- Corners of mouth pulled back or rapid breathing
- Barking*
- Sudden burst of energy
- Animated movements
- Unable to settle – restless
- Panting
- Depression – "shut down" – not reacting to anything, – a dog always seen as being good, but "unnaturally so". This is not to be confused with being relaxed.

Vocal signal which can accompany body language.

Appeasing signals:
used to indicate his intentions are peaceful and no threat:

- Wiggling all over, as if happy, displaying puppy behaviour by an adult dog. Usually the dog has a rounded body with the back end lowering then the front end doing the same.
- Rolling on back to reveal belly
- Jumping up
- Urinating through excitement or fear

Displacement signals:
coping strategies born out of frustration and anxiety:

- Rolling on back to reveal belly
- Digging
- Chewing on something, often the lead
- Tail chasing
- Tugging on clothes
- Biting feet / chewing self
- Scratching
- Jumping up – seeking attention
- Fly catching
- Shadow chasing
- Mounting behaviour
- Strong pulling on lead
- Shivering

Some of these signals would overlap depending on the situation and on the dog.

These lists are examples of what you may see, but they are by no means the full canine repertoire.

Turning away as shown by Poppadom (the goat) and Flitwick (the cat) who accompany us on walks. When a camera is pointed at them they turn away to avoid it, both pretending they've seen something they are interested in. We use the same kind of communication when we want to avoid someone or something; we look the other way, appearing to have a different focus.

Digging; a displacement activity for this dog, but it may not be for another. All situations should be assessed and the action viewed in its proper context.

Street dogs living in Thassos, a Greek island.

Note the signals – paw lift, head dip, turn away (human as well as dogs). My hand is on the white dog's back, which may be the reason why she has dipped her head. If a dog were to put a paw on another's back, it would be seen as a threatening action. Head dipping is a regularly used communication signal. The white dog's mouth is partially relaxed and her tail is semi relaxed, so, although she came to me, she may not be happy with the situation. In the time I knew her, she always used appeasing body language. This is what drew me to her.

Humans

If we are unable to recognise the dog's communication, it is as though the dog is not being heard. A dog will have exhibited a range of signals to indicate he is not happy with what is going on, and probably shown a number of other behaviours too, before reaching the point of biting (which usually catches our attention!).

While we may ignore the mild signs, lacking the education to identify or understand them as being a form of communication, we often punish the dog when they give more overt signals such as – jumping up, growling, baring teeth, lunging, barking, nipping or biting. Have you ever been in the position where no one listens to you and your needs are not catered for? Have you been punished for trying to put your point across? Well imagine this happening daily in all aspects of your life, at work, at home and socially. Ignoring people to this degree can be a form of bullying. What a life! Would you become depressed or possibly turn the opposite way – snap and lose control from time to time? When a dog does this he may very well be put to sleep as a result of his actions. Yet, most dogs DO put up with this deprivation throughout their lives.

Human, goats and cat all communicating, turning away from the camera as if they didn't know I was standing in front of them taking a photo. Every time I pointed the camera at the cat and goats they turned either their heads or their whole bodies away as if interested in something else, when in fact, there was nothing there. Using this behaviour as a distraction, they were avoiding trouble and the intrusion of a strange object being pointed at them.

Key points | Canine communication signals

 Some signals overlap depending on the situation and the dog.

 The dog's communication signals will escalate if he feels he is not being understood.

 We often punish the dog when they give more overt signals such as jumping up, growling, barking, nipping or biting.

 Overt signals are a "last resort" in a dog's repertoire of behaviours. It is perfectly possible to avoid letting things get this far.

Is my dog worried?

Sometimes anxiety is quite obvious, but not always. Once we learn to observe our dogs and recognise their signals, we can identify their worried state early on, giving us a great opportunity to avoid forcing them into situations which they find difficult.

How can we tell if a dog is coping with life?

If the dog has adequate time to recover from each episode of excitement or anxiety, then he is more able to cope with events as they occur.

The time for recovery will vary from dog to dog but remember, in general, they will take longer than many of us allow ourselves to get back on track following the ups and downs in life. While dogs may appear to have recovered quickly from events, this is likely to be superficial, similar to a person putting on a front when feeling vulnerable. It's a survival mechanism. Given the opportunity, many animals, including dogs, usually take life at a slower pace than humans do. Perhaps we can learn and benefit from the valuable lesson they offer us. For most dogs, even fairly regular experiences such as a trip to the vet, a thunderstorm or having lots of visitors coming to their home, may take up to a week to get over.

It is a good idea to do little with the dog for a while after worrying or exciting events, allowing the dog to rest and sleep quietly. Calm walks for no longer than 30 minutes, depending on the type and character of the dog, how he views the world and his state of health. Some dogs can find daily walks an ordeal. Indeed the dog may need even more time to recover from stressful events if he is in poor health – mentally, emotionally or physically. More extreme episodes, like a spell in kennels, being lost, or being the victim of an attack, will require a much longer recovery period.

The low level signals described are in most cases quite normal actions that simply acknowledge what is going on around them, just as we may twiddle our hair, stroke our face and so forth when we are thinking, waiting for something to happen or chatting to someone. Low-level signals often take place when two dogs meet, particularly if both are friendly and sensible.

However, when clusters of signals occur or are made in rapid succession then become stronger and exaggerated, it is likely that the dog is finding things difficult.

Let's go back to the example of the dog being greeted by a person. Some dogs tolerate people's advances less well than others, and such a dog may freeze momentarily at the sight of an approaching stranger. If the person continues, which often they will, due to not seeing a dog standing still as a problem for either of them, the dog may turn away whilst still keeping an eye on the human. If his request for politeness is ignored, the dog may dodge the oncoming person and lower his body as they reach forward in an attempt to stroke him. The dog may try to escape, which will, of course, be impossible if he is on a lead.

This situation is likely to be repeated many times and the dog may test out different tactics such as avoiding people by walking on a curving route or he may try to use barking and, if he is continually put in this same uncomfortable position, his behaviour may escalate to lunging, growling or worse. Not every dog will resort to such displays. There are those who encounter certain triggers on their walks but they learn to put up with them, not that this is fair, but they do.

Let me emphasise that when signals occur in clusters and / or erratically or in quick succession, the dog is almost certainly feeling uncomfortable and is likely to develop stress related issues if something isn't done to address his problems.

If stressful episodes happen occasionally, say once every few months and the dog has recovery time with nothing much going on in between, then he may be able to tolerate this without too much impact on his health and well being, though sadly many owners unknowingly put their dogs under pressure all too often.

Humans

Can we learn to trust our intuition more? When we take on any pet, their welfare is our responsibility and we make judgements on what is in their best interest. If we sense our dog is not comfortable with a person or situation, even if we cannot identify exactly what is prompting our concern, we can take action to protect him. Better to take him away from a potentially stressful experience than to stick it out and hope for the best. Dogs are usually unable to make the necessary changes when difficulties arise in the home or whilst they are at the other end of a lead. We've denied them the option to escape from what is troubling them, so it is our role to help them.

This dog is in a worrying situation, trying to cope by sniffing the floor. Many dogs use sniffing as a distraction, pretending they've not seen something. This dog has to cope in a very difficult environment; with people all around him, nowhere to go and restricted by a tight lead and collar. How must this dog feel? Reverse the situation: how would you cope tied up in a place full of unfamiliar dogs and people who do not understand what you are saying to them? I would be extremely worried about my safety.

Hagrid's favourite communication signals, when things are too much for him, start with a yawn followed by scratching. He scratches often having a skin problem so has learned to use this as a first resort when communicating. He's also had much stress in his early life due to bullying, human commands and shouting, so his stress levels are fairly high anyway as far as people are concerned. When he scratches, I know he is struggling, so, if it's possible, I change the situation either by altering what is bothering him (often related to human activity) or moving him away from the problem.

What can we do? ✋

■ First and foremost, the best thing is to **remove the dog from the situation** without dragging him, which just increases anxiety levels or change the situation as soon as possible, keeping the dog and ourselves calm throughout.

■ **Distracting the dog may work**, although if the dog is already "fixed" it is probably too late. Many dogs need to watch for a while to assess what's going on but, for some, when too close to what concerns them, they may become static or reactive. If the dog is unable to move of his own accord, it is usually better for us to stay calm and grounded; being close by supporting and showing him we can take care of the situation. However, there may be occasions when splitting up could work. This is a natural behaviour dogs use to help each other in difficult situations and, once we have the skills to read the scene safely, we can act in a similar way by walking calmly (without touching or speaking) between the dog and the source of his anxiety. It may take several attempts, but does help many dogs to cope better and to move on.
Unless we have the knowledge and experience to fully assess the scene, avoid actions which risk placing anyone in danger.

■ **Give the dog the space** he needs to deal with what prompts his anxiety. The distance required will vary from dog to dog, as will the situations causing the tension. What one dog finds terrifying may be of little concern to another.

■ Sometimes **simply waiting** until whatever is worrying the dog has gone may be sufficient for him to cope, as long as the dog has adequate space and is not too freaked out (but again, it all depends on the relevant factors and the situation).

■ **Give the dog the time he needs to recover** from events and activities and a tranquil environment in which to do so.

■ **Identify and reduce the stressors and exciting areas** in the dog's life.

■ **Try to avoid putting the dog under the same pressure again,** as behaviour could rapidly deteriorate, potentially leading to biting.

■ If the dog has reached the biting stage then **seek advice** from myself or a member of the Sheila Harper team A.S.A.P. Contact details can be found at the back of the book.

■ The solution may be a combination of several of the above suggestions. **As understanding of canine language grows, the more effectively we can work out what best suits a dog.**

In the pictures on the previous page, Hagrid has the security of a long line. It provides a boundary, preventing him running after farm animals, wildlife, or anything else. If he becomes scared, his reaction may cause him to be viewed as a dangerous dog, but a long line enables me to manage the situation. Many dogs feel safer knowing there are boundaries.

Hagrid had the choice to meet the cows or not. He decided to have a look at them then turned away in his own time. It helped that the cows were calm and approached the gate slowly. Hagrid had not met cows before, but keeping minimal tension on the lead prevented anxiety developing. If I had suddenly tightened the lead, it may have created a charged atmosphere. Hagrid's stress levels were low enough for him not to react but to make a sensible choice. He sniffed the ground and turned away.

In the bottom picture we can see how both the cow and Hagrid mirror one another's body language.

Because I didn't appreciate Kaos' anxiety at a dog show, she had to tell me by running away from the situation. Being the size she was, I had no choice but to listen to her! At this point I still had much more to learn. How many dogs are forced to stay in situations they are unhappy with? She was wearing a choke chain which must have dug into her neck. Dogs often cough and have breathing difficulties as a result of the restriction on their throats and around their necks. Also observe how the man and his mastiff mirror each others' body language. Although you are unable to see his face, I can assure you that he looked just as surprised as his dog.

Key points | Is my dog worried?

 All mammals exhibit a response to stress; it is not necessarily a bad thing. If a dog is given adequate time to recover from an episode of excitement or anxiety (and each dog will have different requirements depending on his character, experiences and other factors) then he is more likely to cope better with events as they occur.

 For most dogs these days, quality rest is probably more important than too much inappropiate exercise. Slow things down, reducing the stress and excitement levels.

 Take notice of your intuition, if something doesn't feel right then it probably isn't.

 Give your dog space and plenty of time to recover from stressful events, as well as avoiding difficult situations.

 Using a fixed (not retracting) long line helps to manage a dog in situations, whilst helping him to feel secure by knowing there are clear boundaries and you are supporting him.

Stress

When communication signals are not effective, dogs begin to show signs of stress. Once we learn how to spot them we can make changes so that the dog has less to worry him. Would you recognise that the adult dog here is not happy with this situation?

Dogs/Humans

A good number of behavioural problems and some health problems associated with dogs are actually caused by living under constant stress – too many demands overwhelming the dog.

Stress is an integral part of any living creature's existence on a daily basis whatever they may do.

We need stress to survive so there's no automatic reason to be worried on seeing the word "stress". Any occurrence either positive or negative can be a stressor. Simply living causes stress on mind and body, but it only creates problems from the resulting chemical changes, when the stressor is sufficiently severe or when incidents are happening frequently with insufficient time to recover in between. We may have a brand new car and look after it incredibly well, but it will deteriorate with use and age. Wear and tear = stress.

The following describes "stress" in short:

Stress triggers the body to produce adrenalin in the presence of short term stressors. Stress that persists needs more adrenal help in the form of cortisol, DHEA (dehydroepiandrosterone) and other factors. These hormones are your body's main defence mechanisms for dealing with stress and should be used sparingly.

In an ideal world, cortisol levels are high in the morning and ease off towards the end of the day. However, when there's a long-term overload of stress, the body requires more cortisol and DHEA but is unable to continue producing enough DHEA, so adverse effects are felt such as an inability to sleep, a weakened immune system, energy slumps during the day or a lack of body temperature control. Stress symptoms create further stress and so begins a vicious cycle. The body needs sufficient time in between each stressful episode to repair itself. How long a period is required will vary from human to human and dog to dog depending on many factors, but is roughly 3-5 days for each event. Dogs have a similar physiological make up to us in this respect, so the same sort of rules are likely to apply to both species.

Above left: The adult dog could easily take control of the stick if he chose to but, instead, continues the interaction rather than using his strength against such a youngster. However, he is displaying some unease indicated by his head being angled away from the pup, ears flat to the head, widened eyes and tension in both face and body.

Stress comes not only from what you do, but also from what you eat. If you, or your dog, frequently eat junk food, low quality food or any foods the body finds difficult to digest, this will also prompt a stress reaction.

Food is a constant factor in dogs' and people's lives and we need to recognise the impact it can have on stress levels.

Even with inert objects stress is a component. Let's say that when carrying a number of heavy boxes they toppled over, spilling onto the ground with one breaking. On further inspection, the broken box had previously been damaged on the opposite side and taped together. Because this box had experienced more stress than the others, it had a greater inherent risk of breakage. We can apply this to life forms too. By keeping stressful events to a minimum and giving adequate time between for the opportunity to recover, we may not "break" as easily, coping better with life in general.

Stress can and does crop up in all sorts of situations – emotional, social, physical and intellectual. Stress also comes from exercise – it is taxing on the body. Now imagine what may happen if you have health problems developing and you are forced to take inappropriate exercise. A great number of dogs are put under this particular stress. It may not be done knowingly, as dogs and other animals don't often exhibit the signs of illness until it has reached a serious stage. Under the rules of "Survival of the Fittest", they are conditioned to know it's unwise to show disabilities or weaknesses.

Dogs as well as people react to the state of mind and moods of those they live with. If we are racing around pushing up our adrenalin levels, we will have an effect on our dogs and other members of the family who may find their stress levels will also rise. Both human and canine species can pick up on the anxiety and the emotional state of the mother whilst still inside the womb. This can and does have an impact on the developing foetus if stress is severe and/or long term.

The litter of pups produced by a bitch experiencing a stressful life will have been affected whilst in the womb and, if the bitch remains fearful and anxious, will continue to influence the pups as she rears them. In humans physical effects such as a greater incidence of children developing asthma have been noted if the mother experiences high stress during her pregnancy. Experiments have already been carried out on animals, showing similar results.

Stress can also be aggravated by fumes, toxins, allergens and many other factors within the environment. Long term stress will affect the way a body copes with these influences.

If high stress is allowed to continue over months or years it can lead to serious health problems, one of which is "adrenal fatigue". It is well worth looking up this topic.

"Adrenal fatigue can affect anyone who experiences frequent, persistent or severe mental, emotional or physical stress. It can also be an important contributing factor in health conditions ranging from allergies to obesity. Despite its prevalence in our modern world, adrenal fatigue has generally been ignored and misunderstood by the medical community".
(Dr James Wilson. *Adrenal Fatigue: The 21st Century Stress Syndrome*)

Dogs

Nowadays, dogs are exposed to an overload of stressful situations on a frequent and regular basis. They experience the demands and high expectations for behaviour and performance from the humans who own them which ensures that, like us, a great many dogs are subject to stress. From personal experience, I know of a number of dogs who are suffering from this condition.

Dogs

Domesticated dogs are far removed from their natural world and this impacts on them greatly. Whilst a degree of evolution has allowed dogs to learn to tolerate small changes, I do believe we have put far too many humanised activities into their lives. Perhaps we can start to think about ways in which we can move into the dog's world instead.

So, what was this natural canine world like? A dog would have lived surrounded by its family, spending much of the time lying around their base, generally not going too far from it, just exploring here and there in the locality to check out what had been going on but at an easy-going pace. Activity for older members of the group would most likely be confined to scavenging and hunting as and when necessary, the rest of the time being devoted to sleeping, resting, sniffing and keeping watch. Apart from feeding and toileting, the puppies would play for brief bursts, explore and examine the immediate environment then SLEEP. Dogs would rush to escape from danger or to hunt food but they rarely ran for the sake of it. We have taught them to chase unnatural things such as balls, frisbees and the like. Influencing behaviour in this way can be (potentially) harmful especially when doing it to excess and it has caused, and is causing, all kinds of problems for them as well as for us, not least because dogs who have become fuelled with adrenalin can suffer withdrawal effects when it ceases. They may develop obsessive behaviour traits and these can cost us a good deal of time, effort and money to sort out. Then there's the physical impact on the dog's health from high level activity and adrenalin production which can prompt early onset of arthritis as well as other diseases.

Sniffing – what dogs do naturally to give them information about the world. Reducing stress levels enables a dog to be able to concentrate and sniff long enough to learn about the environment he is in.

Key points │ Stress

A good number of behavioural problems and some health problems associated with dogs are actually caused by living under constant stress – too many demands overwhelming the dog.

Dogs, like us, react to the state of mind and moods of those they live with.

Long term stress can and does lead to serious health problems.

When a dog has a problem, consider how we can move into the dogs' world and see things from their standpoint.

Share interests and life.

Dogs in a man-made world

Think about the places we take our dogs to. If we take time to learn their language, we have the chance to know whether they really are comfortable in our world, doing the things we think will be suitable for them. We often do things simply because others do but how about questioning why and who it's for.

Dogs/Humans

We often rush around in the presence of our dogs, who are placed at the hub of family life and all that goes with it: phones ringing, music playing, lots of noisy computer games, TVs and radios blaring, people at the door, family squabbles, washing machines, vacuum cleaners, dogs in adjoining gardens (lack of space is something many suffer from), weird smells from cleaning products and air fresheners. You get the idea.

Our moods vary from day to day and so do the dogs', but do we realise when their emotions have changed? Not many of us are aware of variations in our dog's mood, let alone able to do anything about it. Have we the time to care? We're often too busy with our own agenda to recognise what is going on and are not in the position to take action. Sometimes we can become so caught up in all of our own demands it's hard to know how other members of the family are feeling.

To meet their needs, our dogs have to try to sleep amidst this hubbub. Maybe we think they are sleeping, but are they really? Have a close look; is the dog aware of every movement going on around him and has not "switched off"? Some dogs are too stressed to be able to switch off often because they are given far too much exercise, as recommended by so many people these days. Believe it or not, living in this kind of environment is very wearing for a dog. He is constantly alert, waiting for something to happen (which it invariably does).

Because we have so much going on in our lives, we may then feel guilty, thinking we must do more with our dogs. So, what do we do to make it up to them? Perhaps we take them to dog training where they must weave in and out of other dogs and people they are not familiar with, invading another dog's body space or vice versa, which is a very rude thing to do in the dog's eyes. We leave them in a room with a whole host of two and four-legged strangers, whilst we go out, then come back in, expecting them to stay put until WE permit them to move.

Maybe we take them to agility classes, where they can become so wound up they can't stand still and / or they get things wrong, or end up in a fight with another dog because they can't think straight. How about taking them to dog shows so that they can socialise? The more socialisation the better, or so we are led to believe!

Socialisation as it is usually promoted is something I have found actually creates problems. Let's consider a different approach.

The most important thing for any animal (including humans) is that they feel safe and secure in their immediate surroundings and, for dogs, that they can trust their owners and the family. Given a stable foundation to their lives and support from the owner, they will be far more likely to cope with more challenging environments. If we constantly test dogs by exposing them to unnecessary demands and over stimulation provided by people biased activities just because we can, we may set up problems. Is it fair for us to expect any dog to be at ease in the majority of human situations and events? Maybe every now and then according to their experience and skills, but regularly having to endure it is probably something we don't want them to have to do. When you are familiar with canine communication, you are able to recognise the early signs that your dog is finding a challenge too difficult for his current level of social skills, so, if a problem begins to develop, consider going back to basics to rebuild that safe feeling before continuing to add new things into the dog's life or moving him on to further demands. A period of rebalancing tailored to the dog's specific needs will be necessary before you progress.

What is your dog really going to come across in life? Do dogs actually need to go to activities such as the local farmers' market, car boot sales, playing

Training: how I used to do it. I now train dogs in a different way by avoiding testing them and opting for an environment where they are more comfortable.

fields to watch a football match or to the town centre? Why? Who is it for? Take a look at the reasons why we want to take them to places, are they valid or is it just because we want to go and expect the dog to come along too? If a dog is clearly not able to cope, what is the point of exposing him time and again to such stress?

Meeting other dogs is something we would like ours to do comfortably and naturally. Thinking about it in advance but just putting it into practice as and when the situation arises, is likely to be more successful than making an issue of it.

Only when Hagrid felt safe, secure and he trusted me, was he able to learn about other things in his environment. Where I live we frequently come across cows when walking so it was a good idea for him to feel comfortable near them. He was introduced slowly to them, over weeks and months; smelling them in the distance first, briefly seeing them from afar every now and then (not on every walk so he wasn't constantly being moved forward to focus on cows) and gradually, without any fuss, just accepted that they were there, part of the neighbourhood scene.

I suddenly realised that cows were not an issue for him and that is how it happens when you proceed at the dog's pace. It was the same with traffic and meeting people on walks, neither being a part of his life prior to living with us. Come to think of it, even going for walks was new to him. Exposure to these novel experiences was offered as a natural occurrence lasting just a few seconds here and there with occasional longer periods if his communication was low key, indicating that he was able to learn a little more.

Nowadays there appears to be too much emphasis on socialisation, training and having to do things with our dogs. Maybe this is where things have become out of balance. Are we too aware of what is in the media and has the advice issued taken us in the wrong direction? Are we, in effect, trying too hard? Perhaps if we concentrated more on **being** with our dogs, spending quality time with them, simply sitting down and observing them and noticing what they want and like, rather than doing what we want and like, or think we should do, in order to fulfil our expectations of them, then we might have more connected relationships.

Having had first hand experience of creating a problem dog through excessive, inappropriate play and overwhelming her with too much socialisation, I feel there is not enough relevant education and teaching about this area of a dog's development and many owners have only the vaguest idea of what socialisation needs to cover anyway.

The machine was cleaning pavements in a busy local park. Vehicles like this can scare some puppies for life and the rotating brushes can turn on the prey drive for some highly stressed dogs. Just one bad experience like this could prevent a dog from wanting to go for a walk. Children may also become scared by noisy machinery. We are able to explain the working of machines to them but not to dogs.

- We force them to meet every dog, human and animal, so that they will have encountered new experiences.

- We make them walk next to noisy, smelly traffic of all types that heads straight at them.

- We take them on great long walks or runs using short leads which encourage the dog to pull as they are held too close to the owner for comfort; pulling is how they try to create greater space. Or we use extendable leads which often jolt the dog when the brake is suddenly applied, so that there is no warning when a stop is coming.

- We let them loose and make them chase after balls and sticks, over all kinds of terrain, in and out of water and so on for far too long. Dogs weren't born with balls in their mouths and their mothers don't encourage the high level excitement repeated ball chasing causes. We weren't born with cigarettes in our mouths either, but both things are addictive. For a dog that is already reactive to sight, sound and touch, ball play can create further problems. It is a reflex action for a dog to chase something that moves. Some dogs become so full of adrenalin that they begin to chase other moving objects and not just balls.

Dogs having a better balance in life may be able to have a ball thrown every once in a while but it certainly suggests that there is a problem if a dog and / or owner are unable to cope with situations without having a ball with them.

■ **Then, because the dogs can't relax, we assume they aren't worn out yet!** In reality they are probably exhausted, just running on adrenalin, but what do we do when we get them home? We give them more to do, increasing the level of activity rather than reducing the amount of stress.

If a dog is hooked on having a ball thrown for him it can cause added problems when the activity suddenly stops. Where some dogs may cope with instant withdrawal, many will not and, over a period of time, a programme to wean them off their obsession could be employed to ease them through the difficult transition.

In my experience, it can be more difficult for some owners to make the change! Often dogs are happy enough simply carrying a ball and, if they drop it to sniff something in the locality, continuing the walk without giving any attention to the abandoned ball offers a very natural way of progressing towards less dependency. Other dogs who persist with their ball addiction and become agitated if it isn't thrown, could be satisfied by their owner / carer gently rolling the ball along the ground a few times instead of it being thrown at speed. Occasionally there may be an element of frustration and one way to help is by simply 'being' there for the dog, perhaps offering relaxing massage and touch, if the dog can tolerate it but, to soothe the dog, you will need to be in a calm state yourself thus ensuring your influence reduces the dog's arousal.

Because every dog is different it's impossible to cover all eventualities without seeing the individual, though offering occasional opportunities for nose work would certainly be useful but make sure it is done in a sedate manner. If an activity is overused or done in a highly stimulating way, it could be detrimental to the dog's progress, almost like replacing one stimulus with another. Dogs can benefit and do well without these crutches and so can we. It's a matter of learning a different way to be. Consider how it feels when we take part in a pleasurable activity now and then. However, if we partake on a regular basis, does it retain its novelty value?

Think about our own lives. We have a hectic day, then get home to be just as busy with family life, giving us no time to rest. Maybe we do an aerobics class, visit the gym during the evening to "relax", (well it's good for us isn't it?) and then come back home and go to bed.

We may well find it difficult to switch off and sleep at the end of this sort of day, so why expect our dogs to be any different? We rush them around the park on short tight leads, rarely giving them the time they need to sniff or wee at their leisure before dragging them along again because we have so little time before heading off to our next commitment.

Quick, quick, hurry, hurry.

Do you want to live in a world like this?

Given the choice, I'm sure most of us would prefer to take our time, looking at what takes our fancy, occasionally saying hello to a passing person and so on but a number of dogs are somehow expected to take all this tearing around and these demanding schedules, day after day, then we wonder how and why our dog became badly behaved or ill!

I must emphasise that there are some dogs who cope with high level activity better than others and may appear to like training, ball play, agility and other humanised activities we subject them to. However, they may show symptoms of ill health (skin, digestive, and / or joint problems to name a few) or behavioural issues far sooner than they may otherwise have done if they had not been exposed to this type of command-dependent activity.

Controlling animals in this way and on a frequent basis, will inevitably have an effect on them, perhaps leading some to become almost helpless; the dog's spirit is broken in effect. Many will be unable to recover but some dogs are naturally more resilient than others. Among those who have been "crushed" but not "broken" there will be those who, if they are understood, may be in a position to regain their former personalities, providing they have someone available who is caring, supportive, sensitive and concerned about them, giving the time required for that dog to re-establish trust.

It is well worth becoming educated in canine communication before deciding whether your dog likes or dislikes any activities you may wish to share with him.

Being able to "read" a dog will help you in your attempt to understand your dog's needs. If he was a person you wished to have a good relationship with, you would ask him whether he wanted to take part and he would be able to give you an honest response. Understand that your dog can give you an answer in most cases, as well as letting you know when he has had enough of whatever he is doing and would appreciate a break.

To some extent working dogs living outside have advantages over pets that live in the house. Although they may have to do high energy activity at times, most have days off and can make their own choices of how to spend their time. Very often they opt for sleep and rest or just amble around. They aren't subjected to the comings and goings of a busy family life, with all the noise of machinery and entertainment sources that fill most homes. All in all, it may be a more peaceful, balanced life for some working dogs but putting your average pet outside in a kennel isn't the way to go. Many working dogs have become used to their outdoor regime over generations, so to suddenly make changes which deprive a pet dog of the security and familiarity of home would be very harsh.

The lifestyle most of our dogs have is very far removed from living with a few other family members, in the wilderness where for a short time each day they go hunting or scavenging. When on a hunt, dogs survey, listen and sniff intently showing keen interest in gathering information about potential prey that has visited the area recently. They track, moving slowly so as not to spook the game, before a short surge at speed to catch and bring down the prey. It is not a process which can be rushed.

Ideally, our dogs would benefit from between 16 - 18 hours of sleep or quality rest in each day, though a puppy will require even more.

Obviously things can and do go wrong for dogs living naturally. They have stressors such as where is the next meal coming from. Possibly, there won't be one and there may be too many dogs in one area for the available resources. But then they do have choices they can make using brain power, a challenge which our domestic dogs lack. They are rarely given options. We decide for them and the decisions we make are what we think they require not necessarily what is really needed.

Dog sleeping? Sometimes dogs appear to be sleeping but are they really? By giving Hagrid the right environment, and the opportunity to sleep, he can learn it is safe for him to do so when he needs to. By providing appropriate conditions, we are able to offer our dogs the option to sleep during the day as well as at night. Because Hagrid is calm the cat chooses to doze close to him, however he had to learn how to sleep and relax.

Our choices are often based on what everyone else is doing with their dogs and how they do it. This is usually guided by media and fashion so we follow and do it too, but are there other ways we might explore?

Many people still apply outdated practices. For example, the theory of dominance hierarchy was put forward, a number of years ago, by L David Mech, senior scientist and authority on wolves (*www.davemech.com*). However, since then, he has admitted that mistakes were made and is now trying to eradicate dominance theory from public awareness. So perhaps it is time to look at the dogs we have today for the answers rather than carry on using discredited ideas. Since changing the way I work, I have been in a better position to see what my dogs did and didn't like or understand and the effect my actions have on them.

What a difference it's made; I am now open to them, enabling honest interaction with me. Any fear has gone and they feel safe to communicate, confident of being heard, understood and respected for what they say.

If we are asked to consider doing something in a different way, we may be fearful of trying it, but in order to benefit dogs, it would be helpful if more people were open minded and took a fresh look at dog training.

When dogs are subjected to prolonged stress, is it surprising how frequently we start to see health issues developing in them? Often infections and digestive or skin problems are early signs. Body shape can also change and the dog's outline looks different. Behaviour problems are another common sign of stress.

Often dogs suffering prolonged stress develop physical issues such as a roached (rounded) back and/or their hind quarters tuck underneath them. Alternatively, the back legs become very stiff and straight.

If symptoms are showing on the outside then things are probably much worse on the inside. The dog's body is not coping with the amount of stress it is experiencing.

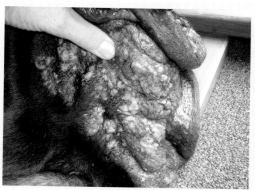

Acne, just one of the stress-related skin problems Hagrid brought with him.

A dog with too hectic a schedule may not have the opportunity to digest his food properly or, to a large extent, may even lose interest in eating. I know this from experience, but fortunately for my dog, once the stress had been dramatically reduced in her life, she could enjoy her meals as opposed to picking at the contents of her bowl before walking away. She moved on from being an underweight mastiff to a well proportioned one who felt relaxed in her home. On the other hand, some highly stressed dogs may feel the need to gobble down their food, which can be similarly damaging to the digestive process. If we take a look at ourselves: when we are anxious and going through a stressful patch, we may either have no appetite or we want to consume everything in sight, often not feeling fully satisfied, hence the need to eat and eat in an attempt to fill an emotional gap. What we are aiming for, in ourselves and our dogs, is a balance.

When we have eaten a lovely meal in a relaxing situation, without a care in the world, not having to rush off anywhere afterwards, it is all too easy to fall asleep, or at least feel like it. If we are lucky, maybe we can sit around for an hour or so, savouring the moment. Resting after a meal aids digestion so would be the ideal, as is taking things at a slow pace before moving on to the next item on the agenda. If there isn't adequate stress-free time available to process food, there is a risk for long term digestive disorders to manifest.

A stressed dog cannot digest its food effectively and is equally liable to develop problems.

So, if you see dogs who are either very poor eaters or wolf down their food, consider their anxiety or stress levels and what you might be able to do to help. There are a number of dogs who even refuse treats in certain settings which could be an indication of how the dog is feeling in that particular place. On the other hand some dogs will go on to eat anything in sight, including bizarre and quite inappropriate items. As anxious people can have eating disorders, so can dogs.

Key points | Dogs in a man made world

 Modern western society functions at an unnaturally fast and hectic pace.

 Our moods might vary from day to day but do we allow for this in our dogs?

 Because most of us are busy, we tend to assume that keeping our dogs busy is good for them but it is all too easy to overwhelm a dog with an excess of various types of exercise, training and / or socialisation.

 Spending time simply being with our dogs could be better for them.

 Long term adrenalin overload in dogs may well cause health problems, which can be indicated by their body language.

 Good relationships between people allow both to have a say on what they choose to do together. We can give our dogs the chance to tell us what they like to do with us by learning to read their body language.

 Dogs need more rest and sleep than most people realise; at least 16 hours a day.

Warning signs

When communications are not listened to or get no response, the language becomes louder. We can help our dogs before they reach more extreme warning signs.

Dogs

Signs of stress

Some of these indicators also overlap other lists.

Signs of stress are shown through body language signals as, the dogs are communicating how they feel, to us.

- Shaking
- Freezing
- Growling
- Nipping
- Biting
- Shivering
- Weeing

- Not weeing
- Drinking obsessively
- Not drinking
- Eating hurriedly
- Not eating
- Lethargy
- Manic activity

Two dogs who live together communicate their good intentions. Jaffa's body is curved away as is Hagrid's head, both indicating they mean no harm to the other. This is not just a comfortable way of lying down, they are communicating.

Be aware that a dog lying head-on to another one could be using bullying tactics. It's a subtle action and must be assessed in context.

Dogs living together have to work hard on a daily basis to maintain amicable relations.

They very often have little time away from the others. My dogs sleep in different areas of the house at night as well as having separate walks during the day. They have the choice of more than one room and various flooring options.

Dogs

Causes of anxiety that may be overlooked

What is likely to worry a dog depends on many factors such as the situation, the dog's personality, health and previous experience, as well as the dog's current adrenalin and arousal levels.

The impact of an occurrence will also vary depending on the time of day and whether the dog is tired or not. It is exactly the same if we have had a day where events have irritated us and we have not had much sleep (having other worries on our mind) then things which previously wouldn't be of concern suddenly begin causing us to react. Feeling a little under the weather, having odd aches and pains or some illness brewing can make anyone feel more irritable and snappy. **So if you have a reactive dog, chances are they are under too much pressure** in some way at that time. People often complain about their dog being unpredictable – I can guarantee the dog's behaviour is almost always entirely predictable, providing we have the knowledge to understand what the animal is feeling.

Humans

Being a different species, to fully appreciate the dog's state of mind is probably beyond us, but, given the will to learn about canine body language, we can come so much closer to them. I am not blaming owners for not getting the picture. I am simply requesting that everyone who takes on the responsibility of a dog is educated in the canine communication system, studying it in as much depth as they can.

I believe this to be the greatest thing we can do to change dogs' lives today, to be able to then help them have a better future. Owners CAN do something to make improvements in the vast majority of cases.

Most caring dog owners would welcome a chance to gain knowledge which will make such a difference to their pets. In an ideal world, before taking a dog on, wouldn't it be great if potential owners thoroughly considered whether they have empathy and can spare enough time to learn to understand them? In my view, understanding is definitely an essential component of the dog's welfare.

It is a big commitment affecting many aspects of life, to have a dog become part of your family. Isn't it worth taking plenty of time to think seriously about how a dog is going to impact on daily life and whether it will be suitable for everyone before making any decision?

Dogs/Humans

Dogs check out the environment with their eyes, ears and noses working in unison to make sense of what's going on.

The following can cause anxiety in dogs:

Smells - A dog's ability to detect scent is far more powerful than we can comprehend. They rely heavily on their sense of smell for survival, their prime sensory organ being the nose. A few triggers are:

- Other animals (some breeds will be more susceptible)
- Bitches in season
- Cigarette smoke
- Pollution
- Smell of food (especially if hungry)
- Perfumed products (for humans and dogs)

Some people are physically affected by strong smells triggering things like nausea, migraine and asthma, so what about the much more sensitive canine olfactory system?

Dogs roll in nasty smelly things (Calvin Canine!) and we are repulsed by them. Maybe dogs are repulsed by the scents which delight us. Our noses aren't as efficient as theirs so I wonder what our perfumes smell like to a dog? Of course dogs are unable to bath us or escape from our odour.

Because dogs prefer different smells to us, could we consider reviewing some of the highly perfumed products we use in our homes, making the place more comfortable for our dogs to live in?

Communication problems

- Not being understood
- Barking (for what reason?)
- Not feeling safe and secure
- Pulling on lead
- Devices used to 'control' unwanted behaviour, e.g. spray collars, electric shock collars, pinch harnesses, muzzles and so on. Before using such devices on my dog, I might try it out on myself then decide whether to put it on him. I don't necessarily recommend this action but strongly advise that you imagine what it really feels like for the dog when such equipment is applied before subjecting him to it.

Jaffa taking her time to delicately sniff out information from her environment.

Hagrid, presenting me with a paw lift; a clear indication in this situation for me to go away.

Touch

- Flooring – having to constantly walk on slippery surfaces. Have you tried walking in high heels on laminate flooring or polished ceramic tiles?
- Never knowing when someone will touch them, even when resting and sleeping. Many owners allow anyone to touch the dog, though I'm sure they would be far less keen for people to randomly touch them or their children. What effect might such actions have on us or our children?
- Equipment we put on dogs – collars and harnesses, especially if badly fitting. Also head collars, pinch harnesses, shock collars or choke chains.
- Dressing them up in doggie clothes.
- Being groomed (also no choice, over timing, smell, sight or sound)

Jaffa intensely dislikes being groomed. Grooming takes place in stages: one day I will cut hair from her feet, another day trim her nails, a few days later the clippers will be used and so on until the job is done. Grooming in this way gives her short bursts of stress as well as time to get over each session. She no longer pants, salivates or becomes over excited as she used to when going to the groomers. She can be seen here communicating by using a shake off as I groom her.

No Choice

Much of what we do with dogs, expecting them to endure without complaint, gives them no alternatives.

When we are able to make choices on their behalf, we could make it better for them and when we are unable to do so, we can still recognise that there may be an impact on our dogs. Here are a few scenarios to consider:

- Hunger, thirst, too hot, too cold
- Lack of opportunity to toilet (if restricted to one room all day, this could be reality for a dog)
- Socialisation/training classes
- Dancing with dogs – no choice (did the dog invite you to waltz?)
- Being judged, i.e. dog shows
- "Cani X" and similar activities where the dog is fixed to a person or object. Even when your dog accompanies you on a run, he may feel compelled to keep up rather than risk the vulnerability that goes with being left behind
- Being shut in a car
- Being left alone for hours
- Having to accompany owner everywhere
- Spending too much or too little time with their owner
- Short lead, preventing use of their natural instinct to check out their environment
- Other restrictive equipment
- Other dogs – meeting when out and about
- Exercise – over, under or any inappropriate for the dog at that time
- No resting place where they are left in peace
- Having to live or share with another dog and/or other animals
- Living with family members who are unwilling to understand the dog, or in some cases don't even like the species
- Being housed in the wrong environment; such as a Great Dane living in a top floor flat
- Too much freedom
- No boundaries
- Alterations to routine
- Not having a routine
- Too rigid a routine
- Illness or departure of any member of family, including other animals
- Holidays, whether the dog is with you or not; it's a change
- Trauma for the family, e.g. death, redundancy or unemployment
- Moving house

Showing Kaos (my first Mastiff) using restrictive equipment, leaning over her, forcing her to stay whilst a stranger handled her, as well as having a camera pointed in her face. She was traumatised at Crufts by everything and was totally overwhelmed.

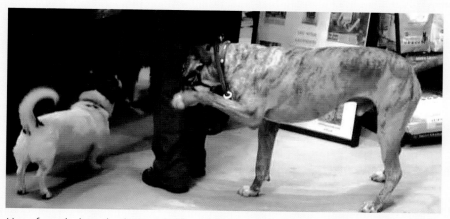

How few choices do these dogs have? They are unable to escape from the situation, restrained by highly restrictive equipment, surrounded by people, they have no personal space or toileting options. They are vulnerable to strangers approaching. Owners and the equipment used exert complete control, imposing the wishes of the owner on the dogs.

Noises

- Fireworks
- Children
- Celebrations
- Arguments
- Alarms
- Radio/Televisions or computer games (which is also sight)
- Sirens
- Refuse/recycling collectors, postmen; anyone at the door
- Traffic (which is also sight)
- Road works, building work in the home and / or vicinity
- Being nagged, too many demands or being shouted at
- Power tools e.g. lawn mowers (which is also sight)
- Thunder or strong winds

Dogs living with children need time and space away from them to be able to rest and relax. For the safety of both children and dogs, good early education is vital and I consider it advisable that they are never left together without a responsible adult in attendance.

The best scenario for dogs and children to spend time with each other is when all is peaceful and the child is absorbed in a calm, quiet occupation, though take care if food or certain types of toys are present. These can create problems for some, depending on various factors including how arousing or worrying the dog finds them.

The dog will probably take frequent looks at the child because, being a mini human, he or she will be different to an adult in the dog's eyes. There are children who can be great around dogs some of the time, especially when they've had guidance from adults who understand both the child's and dog's perspectives but, even so, both will require regular breaks from one another. Remember they are children and can of course behave randomly and be unpredictable – making strange noises and quick, erratic movements, being intense around a dog and often invading his personal space for far too long; this can be especially so with the very young but, when the parent and child are focused on an activity, the dog will more than likely lose interest and lie down somewhere.

Dogs can show symptoms similar to jealousy so remember the need to spend quality one to one time with both child and dog separately.

Gradually, however, as they learn to trust and respect one another, with the parents overseeing matters and intervening when needed, providing support and appropriate boundaries for both, they can build a mutually rewarding and wonderful relationship. Children who learn consideration for animals and about giving choices to other sentient beings, are in the best position to develop respect for all living things. These are valuable skills a child can take through life with them. Learning to adapt to another's needs is part of survival as well as good social behaviour.

Even when relationships between a dog and child are going smoothly, I would add that there is a need for more protection at times when excitement and emotions are high. It can be common for a dog to get worried (and therefore potentially more reactive) by some family events – Christmas, parties, having visitors, arguments and so forth but, by giving the dog a safe area where he can relax undisturbed maybe even somewhere out of the house, he's likely to feel more secure and be less affected. If he is contented resting in a car / van etc, why not use that occasionally, but obviously only if weather conditions mean it will be comfortable and it's safe to do so. Although dogs can and do get used to things, having the resource of one or more safe places can be invaluable. If used with thought and planning, they can help the dog avoid being drawn into family "stuff" he doesn't need to be involved with.

Sight

- Passers by – access to windows and doors
- People always being visible
- Cats, birds, squirrels in the garden or animals on television
- Postmen, window cleaners and so on (which is also noise)
- Overactive owner or or other people in the household
- Cyclists, skateboarders and so on
- Wheelchairs, crutches or walking sticks
- Road sweepers (which is also noise)
- People in hats, hoods, motor cycle gear or unusual clothing
- People carrying items which obscure recognition of the normal human outline such as umbrellas, bags and rucksacks
- Statues
- Restricted or failing vision may cause more problems with objects being distorted; the dog doesn't see clearly which could give rise to them having insecurity and other behavioural issues that weren't noticeable before.

Dogs are subjected to these experiences and a great deal more without any advance knowledge of our communication system and we expect them to handle it without us having to learn their language. How fair is this?

It is so important to offer our dogs suitable options for them to choose from, just as we would for a human being, to help them deal with what must, to them, be an alien environment. If we aren't prepared to develop a two-way relationship with our dogs, maybe it's time to consider whether it's fair for us to keep them as a companion.

I fully acknowledge that dogs and people belong to two different species, but the more science discovers about dogs, the more similarities and parallels are found in physiology, body chemistry and, yes, emotional responses. To me it goes without saying "treat other living beings with the respect they deserve". Therefore, thinking how you might feel before imposing something on your dog may be a good rule of thumb and help you to develop a better relationship with your canine companion.

Key points | Warning signs

 An overactive or lethargic dog may well be responding to stimuli we are not aware of.

 Many things can trigger a reaction e.g. smell, touch, noise, vision and lack of choice.

 Learning to observe and read canine body language is perhaps one of the most useful things you can do for your dog.

 Dogs, like humans, need to have choices in order to help them deal with life.

Choice or Control?

This dog has no choice. They don't control us; we influence dogs' lives. Let's work toward understanding them and sharing communication.

Dogs/Humans

Allowing children to emulate the behaviour of sensible calm adults gives them confidence, enabling them to make good decisions in life.

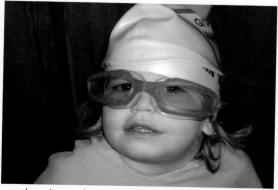

The word no is used too often with children and dogs. How do you feel when someone continually says 'no' to you? For me, it takes away confidence.By giving both dog and child choices, they are more responsive and willing to accept boundaries when necessary so less likely to get into trouble.

Why would I say no to my grand-daughter wanting to wear my swimming hat and goggles? Sometimes we almost automatically say no, without thinking things through properly, as we may have our mind on something else, or we are rushed or agitated. I could ask "why don't people let their dogs make the choice when they want to go in a particular direction or lie in another place?" To me it seems obvious to let the dog make decisions at certain times, especially when on a walk (their walk!) but the number of people who don't allow them to make the simplest of choices such as opting to stop and sniff is so sad. I used to be one of those people, following the crowd without questioning, but can see now how I was.

Before laying down the law to prevent my dogs from doing a particular thing, I simply ask myself "is there any reason why they should not?" Usually I allow my dogs freedom to act, providing it is within the boundaries I have set for them. This has transformed my relationship with my dogs, and more importantly, theirs with me. It is equally possible for anyone to attain similar enlightening experiences when they learn how to understand a dog effectively and make appropriate changes to routines and lifestyle, which will better suit his needs.

The picture on page 35 gives the impression that Hagrid was about to bite my granddaughter, whereas in reality as these pictures show, they were peacefully interacting. It is important to look at the "big" picture, not just one behaviour in isolation and not jump to conclusions.

Communication is a vital component of survival; every species has a right to be understood. We have taken over our dogs' lives in such a massive way. Many would have us believe that this is what they have done to us, which, if you think about it, is rather bizarre. When examining the facts, clearly it's the other way round. Where the dog lives and with whom they share their lives; when, where and what they eat; when, where and for how long they sleep; when and where they toilet; when to exercise, what type and how long for, even their walking speed is invariably determined by us. For pedigree dogs we even decide who they mate with, when and where. Basically, every aspect of a dog's life is controlled by us. Surely the least we can all do in return is to try to understand them, not just the vocal side of things but the silent communication (body language) too, and look at things from their perspective instead of always from our own. Take the information offered; spend time just being with dogs and observing them, that way we can really learn about how they are feeling in the different situations in which they are put. We will then be in the position to help them, rather than expecting them to always fit into our world. Be compassionate and give dogs some choices and simple pleasures in life which are appropriate for them. Let's try and lessen the distress of being misunderstood and ignored.

Like many others who live and work with dogs, I want to understand and learn more about them. This is what most of us aim to do in other relationships we form; we like to know how and what the other person is feeling. Once we realise they don't like, say, football we don't insist on them watching it and playing it day in day out. Even if that is something we enjoy doing, we might avoid or at least limit it when they are around to please them.

People in a successful relationship have respect for the feelings of one another. By reading this book I hope you have become aware that this can apply to dogs too; have consideration for their wants and needs in a similar way as you would a friend. I am overwhelmed by the effectiveness of this knowledge and am confident that both my dogs and I are the happiest we have ever been because of acknowledging my mistakes and letting go of control. Instead, I've learnt to trust, understand and respect dogs and that gives a feeling of great pleasure and satisfaction. I can't emphasise this message enough, and hope you too will enjoy the delights that unfold as you begin to really live with your dogs.

Key points | Choice or Control?

  Communication is a vital component of survival for any living being.

 We can all learn more about how dogs communicate with us.

 Offering appropriate choices provides better long-term results than trying to control your dog. Giving choices helps build brain connections as well as a dog's confidence, so aiding effective decision making.

 Think before making demands on your dog; is it really necessary?

Acknowledgements

First I would love to thank everyone – family, friends, fellow students and advisors of dog behaviour – who have helped me on my journey, **Sheila Harper and Winny Boerman** being at the forefront. What an amazing talent you have for teaching. Thanks for not only improving my dogs' lives but also totally changing mine (for the better!). I am indebted to you along with many other people and dogs whose lives have been transformed by your teachings.

Turid Rugaas – for identifying how dogs communicate via 'calming signals', highlighting the various ways in which we can interact with them: a series of truly amazing breakthroughs that can change the way we are around dogs. I must also congratulate Turid for the gift she has of making it all sound so simple, *when it is!* Trouble is we often like to complicate it all with science and academic words.

Marilyn Aspinall – who has done much editing and re-editing, giving me confidence and courage to follow through stress reduction and management techniques with my Mastiff, Hagrid. Rehabilitating Hagrid has proved to be challenging, but oh so rewarding. It's always more difficult to work with your own dogs as emotions get in the way. Marilyn complements me well with her patience (when I keep updating my thoughts), methodical approach, rationality, organisation and planning. Through working on this book I have come to trust Marilyn implicitly and we have become great friends. Thanks for sticking with it and me.

Jean Gough – for your assessment and views from another angle, and truly welcome remarks, which may have made the book longer, but also hopefully, clearer! Of course, when it comes to dogs, I could go on forever and at times it seemed that's just what I did.

Colin – my ever loyal, loving husband, who has had bags of patience with all the interruptions in his life and the endless: "Colin, can you check this please?" At the outset, like the rest of my family, Colin was sceptical about my change of approach towards the dogs, thinking it was just a fad of mine. Over the months and years, Colin has come to recognise this is a way forward, not just in helping dogs but for all animals, as opposed to my previous backward steps in trying to control their lives. Colin is always full of encouragement and helped me to realise the need for these practices to be known by a wider public.

Jaffa and Hagrid – thanks for the invaluable information, through your communication and the wonderful relationship we now have. To all the dogs who have come into my life one way or another: I am sorry for not understanding at the time, as well as being thankful to all who tried, through their language, to show me the right direction. Now I am open minded, I am able to help dogs and owners alike to progress.

More acknowledgements:

Writing and producing this book has been a great experience, mainly due to the willingness of some lovely people who want to help others understand this better way of working with dogs. They too have had their eyes opened and realise the need for change in the world we share with our companions whether canine or human. There are many wonderful people who have been so supportive of me whilst writing this book and I would like to mention a few of them, thanking them for their contributions:

James Aspinall – a big thank you for helping with boxes! and many superb photographs.

Gerd Köhler – for allowing me to use many of his quality photographs and his willingness to help.

Adrian Jackson – the most patient, organised, skilled graphic designer (and the rest) in the world. I do hope you will work with us again. Maybe we'll have a plan next time!

Jason Penn – the first graphic designer who tried to help us make a booklet, which quickly turned into a book. Again, thanks for your patience, as we struggled to learn more about how to work with a graphic designer!

Jeremy Bassett – who, through his love of working with dogs in this way offered his wonderful skills in marketing to help get this valid (and vital) information out into the public domain.

Thank you all so much.

About me

Throughout my life I have been surrounded by and worked with a broad range of animals (including several dogs!) and ran my own successful pet-sitting business. I've gained several qualifications in animal care, management and handling as well as completing Sheila Harper's IPACS (Parts 1 & 2) - International Programme for Applied Canine Studies (formally IDBTS). However, the far more important outcome of these years of experiences has been the richer understanding I've acquired from learning to look with fresh eyes. My views about animals have been transformed, enabling more meaningful relationships to evolve because of the changes in my perspective and attitude.

When writing this book I was the proud owner of Jaffa, a Cavalier King Charles Spaniel who, previously, had belonged to a pet-sitting client whose circumstances had changed and Hagrid, a rescued English mastiff who, when I had him, was in very poor health, nervous and would have been perceived as a potentially "dangerous dog". They have taught me so much, as have all my dogs.

I am now able to help my dogs have a better quality of life due to all I've gained from the IDBTS (IPACS) course and working with Sheila Harper. I only wish I had known what I know now 20 years ago.

Having had previous experience of many different types of training and behavioural methods, most of which relied on exercising some form of dominance or control over the dog, I realised that they only produced short-term results or made matters worse. After attending further courses, run by Sheila and other similarly enlightened people, I am now able to use my knowledge and experience to help others understand their dogs, work with them to develop a positive relationship, deal with existing issues and prevent other problems developing by putting the ideas and methods I promote into practice.

*A good relationship consists of understanding, sharing and trust.
This shared relationship lays down a solid foundation for a rewarding
partnership to flourish, encouraging problems to dissolve naturally.*

If you'd like to have similarly life enhancing experiences with your dogs please act now for yours and your dog's sake. Enjoy the two way relationship that is built on choices and appropriate boundaries.

Observe yourself and your dog as you both discover the freedom letting go brings.

Since starting to write the first edition of this book back in 2010, two important characters are no longer with us. Jaffa had a number of breed-related diseases which beset Cavaliers; one more victim of the way we continue to influence and control dogs' lives, in this instance, trying to produce an idealised dog without due regard to health. As a result of Mitral Valve Disease, Jaffa was put to sleep on February the 1st 2011. She was a wonderful soul; a sweet natured girl, sensitive and eager to please. Eventually she learnt it was okay to be herself, once I had found out how to implement boundaries without imposing control, commands or demands.

Hagrid's life sadly came to an end on June the 5th 2015 aged eight and a half. After a short acute illness he was put to sleep.

He came to us as a two and a half year old rescued English Mastiff who was in a very poor state. At times, when he was anxious and distressed, he could well have been thought of as a "dangerous dog" but because he was treated with compassion, understanding and empathy, he was no longer seen like that. No one who knew him in the early days thought he'd make the grand age of eight and a half. We certainly didn't expect that ourselves when he came to live with us but, unbelievably, his health improved as he aged. It was quite an incredible journey we were privileged to have been part of and we feel so blessed to have shared our lives with him.

Until we met up with Kuzu (see below), Pogo was our newest edition and again it's incredible to have seen the transformation in her over the few years she's been with us. She's delightful in every way and has livened us up with her bouncy nature. She really was like a coiled spring to begin with, without any etiquette inside the house whatsoever. But now that she feels safe and secure, she's much more laid back and can enjoy her life. Like all my dogs, past and present, she has taught me so much.

And finally we are lucky enough to have found Kuzu, who is half Anatolian Shepherd dog in combination with mastiff mix and American Staffordshire terrier. He's young, big and energetic. Pogo chose him as Jaffa had chosen Hagrid. She had no qualms about going straight up to meet him then calmly choosing to move away, though meeting so quickly hadn't been part of my strategy for their first encounter! Plans are great but they may not always happen.

Pogo relaxing on holiday, enjoying the aroma of the sea air, a novel experience for her.

Kuzu who is a young inexperienced dog, watches and learns about life from a comfortable distance.

For the first few weeks at home, Kuzu and Pogo saw one another from the other side of dog gates until Kuzu had calmed down enough for her to be with him for a short time and we're building up their contact slowly according to both dogs needs at any one time. They and we are learning to integrate Kuzu into our household and he's doing really well, though does have some way to go! He's not had many (if indeed any) boundaries before. Several months on, all of us are now getting more sleep with far fewer disruptions at night, which is bliss. He's learning to respect Pogo's space and boundaries and we're helping both of them. It's akin to having children and teaching them how to be 'nice' to one another but at the same time the parents need to be attentive to the individual's needs. Another new and exciting adventure is happening. Watching them develop is enlightening.

We still miss Jaffa and Hagrid so very much, they were a big part of our family. I'm glad I learned how to give them the chance to change their lives, become the dogs they were but dared not show. Altering how and what I was doing, giving each of them the opportunities to make choices to meet their individual needs, enabled them to grow and rediscover their true character and spirit.

And, finally, I hope that this new perspective can also begin to transform your lives and the dogs you live with.

Further information and reading

Below are a few of the people I have gained much knowledge from.
I hope you will too. Please look them up:

Sheila Harper
www.sheilaharper.co.uk

Turid Rugaas
www.turid-rugaas.no/ukfront.htm

Winkie Spiers
www.winkiespiers.com

Professor Marc Bekoff
http://literati.net/Bekoff/

Barry Eaton
www.deaf-dogs-help.co.uk

Martha Knowles
https://www.facebook.com/silentcanineconversations

my website
www.laidbackdogs.com